Other books by Victor Paul Wierwille

Power For Abundant Living
Receiving The Holy Spirit Today
The Bible Tells Me So
The New, Dynamic Church
The Word's Way
Are The Dead Alive Now?

JESUS CHRIST IS not GOD

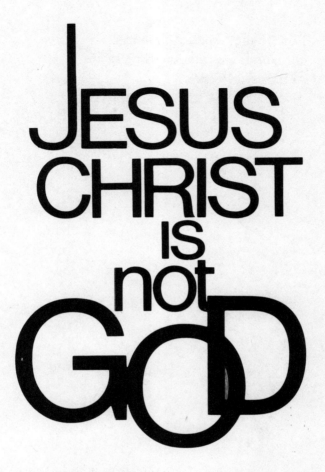

VICTOR PAUL WIERWILLE

THE AMERICAN CHRISTIAN PRESS
New Knoxville, Ohio
Trade Distributor:
The Devin - Adair Co.
Old Greenwich, Conn.

Note to the reader: All biblical
quotations are from the King James
Authorized Version.

Standard Book Number: 0-910068-07-0
Library of Congress Catalog Card Number 74-25962
The American Christian Press
New Knoxville, Ohio 45871
© 1975 by The Way International
Published 1975
Printed in the United States of America

To my wife, Dorothea, who is a loving helpmate to me, a gentle mother to our five children, and an enthusiastic supporter of the ministry to which God has called us. She is a virtuous woman.

ACKNOWLEDGMENTS

I am grateful to many dedicated people for the assist-
ance given to me in preparing and producing this
book. Rev. Walter Cummins and a small research team
worked closely with me after I had once done the basic
research. They also studied all the pro-trinity positions
and discussed them with me. Bernita Jess checked
Aramaic manuscripts when related to the topic, while
Rev. Cummins and Donna Randall checked the Greek.
Ronald G. Webster's research contributed greatly to the
first chapter, "The Origin of the Three-In-One God."

Donna Randall and Karen Wierwille Martin (my editor
and daughter) and my wife, Dorothea, reworked and
proofed the manuscript for readability and clarity. I
thank them knowing how much the readers will benefit
from their efforts.

I acknowledge a very great debt to my secretary, Rhoda Becker Wierwille, who not only typed and retyped this manuscript with a willing heart, but who has been faithful to my secretarial needs for over twenty-five years. To her I am indeed grateful on all counts.

I am grateful to all workers at The American Christian Press, under the leadership of Milford Bowen, and the Way International Bookstore, under the leadership of Emogene Allen, for seeing this book become a concrete reality in its publication and distribution. To all these and many more for their devotion to God's accurate Word, I give thanks.

CONTENTS

JESUS CHRIST IS **NOT** GOD

No statement to many Christians could be more emo-
tionally charged than that of "Jesus Christ is not
God." I can understand this. I was reared in a Christian
denomination that taught the Godhead as a trinity: that
is, "God the Father, God the Son, God the Holy Spirit."
I accepted this doctrine because I respected the sincerity
of my teachers, although its meaning kept vexing my
mind. I vividly recall asking my saintly pastor when I
was just 16 years old to explain the trinity to me. Ever
since then I have searched to understand this doctrine
which has been considered the cornerstone of Christianity for the past fifteen centuries.

I have had access to and have read the major works in
systematic theology both of the past as well as current
publications. For years I have done my utmost in evalu-

ating whatever I could find to read plus directly studying with biblical scholars. I have asked theologians of
unblemished character to discuss the trinity with me,
yet I never found more substance than what my child-
hood pastor, Dr. L. H. Kunst, told me 42 years ago: "No
one can explain the trinity. We simply accept it by faith."

I am aware of the scripture which tells us that God
hasn't revealed all his secrets.

Deuteronomy 29:29:
The secret *things belong* unto the Lord our God: but those
things which are revealed belong unto us and to our children
for ever, that *we* may do all the words of this law.

But I also know that God has revealed to us all things
that pertain to life and godliness.

II Peter 1:3:
According as his divine power hath given unto us all things
that *pertain* unto life and godliness, through the knowledge of
him that hath called us to glory and virtue.

So while studying God's Word for the past several
decades, I have always kept the trinity in mind, hoping
I would find the key to understanding it, hoping that
this wasn't one of God's secrets.

But, through the years, the more and more I carefully
researched God's Word for knowledge, the less and less I
found to substantiate a trinity. Even though I had

always accepted the idea of a three-in-one God, I continually found evidence in the Word of God which undermined a Christian trinity.

If 42 years ago or 30 or maybe even 20 years ago someone had postulated to me that Jesus Christ was not God, I too would have been taken back. But for me it has been a gradual learning and, therefore, an unlearning process as I've progressively gained a knowledge of God and His Son.

I didn't begin research of this topic from a negative framework. It was never part of my motivation to disprove the trinity. If the Bible had taught that there is a Christian trinity, I would have happily accepted it. Obviously, when a person does unpreconceived research, he does not determine beforehand what he will find. Research doesn't begin with the answers; it looks for the answers. I did not willfully choose to find what I have found. Also, my conclusion therefore is no Johnny-come-lately idea set forth to be iconoclastic, splashy or controversial. I have written up my years of research not to be argumentative; neither am I apologetic. I simply want to set forth my study as a workman for God, realizing that if the research is a right-dividing of God's Word, many who believe will be blessed. If my research is a wrong-dividing of God's Word, then I stand before God as an unapproved workman. Either way I accept full responsibility. I have checked God's Word hundreds of times over, and thus I am convinced beyond a shadow of a doubt that Jesus Christ is not God but the Son of God. If I weren't totally persuaded, I wouldn't think of committing this thesis to paper.

I realize that I am asking a great deal of the readers of this study. For what it has taken me several decades to search out in God's Word, I am exposing you to in a moment's reading. What I have had time to think over and pattern through God's Word, you are seeing in rapid progression. What I have had to unlearn from my religious upbringing and culture, you are facing stark naked. In other words, I've had time to study and change my conceptions when necessary. You too will need more time than one reading of the research contained in this volume allows. After all, research doesn't mean a simple, cursory reading; it denotes study, observation and unemotional detached consideration. A topic so utterly important as God and His Son Jesus Christ certainly deserves both yours and my clearest and best thinking.

Before we proceed further, we must define our terms. Many people may be misled because while using the same language or words, we don't mean the same thing. First of all, let me give the orthodox definition of Christian trinity. The doctrine of the trinity states that the Father is God, the Son is God, the Holy Spirit is God and together, not exclusively, they form one God.

The trinity is co-eternal, without beginning or end, and co-equal.[1]

That defines the doctrine of the trinity, and this I do not believe the Bible teaches. With all my heart I believe the Bible teaches that (1) God is the Father of our Lord Jesus Christ, that (2) Jesus Christ is the Son of God and that (3) God is Holy and God is Spirit.

The term "Son of God" is used at least 50 times in the Bible; not one place is there "God the Son." To say that "Son of God" means or equals "God the Son" totally negates the rules of language, leaving it utterly useless as a tool of communication.

In other words, I am saying that Jesus Christ is not God, but the Son of God. They are not "co-eternal, without beginning or end, and co-equal." Jesus Christ was not literally with God in the beginning; neither does he have all the assets of God. The research in this book will show why I believe as I do.

Perhaps many Christians have never questioned or given thoughtful consideration to the doctrine of the trinity. The idea is so well-rooted among church-going and Bible-believing Christians that we've seldom considered the implications of a three-in-one God. What difference does it make whether Jesus Christ is God or

---

1. William Wilson Stevens, *Doctrine of the Christian Religion* (Grand Rapids: Wm. B. Erdmans Publishing Co., 1967), pp. 113-122.

the Son of God? The difference and the importance of this difference is the basic reason for writing this book. *If Jesus Christ is God and not the Son of God, we have not yet been redeemed.* The difference is that important, that critical.

As a preliminary to research let us note that the Bible says there are two types of doctrine: man-made doctrine — what man's mind has thought up or concluded; and God-breathed doctrine — that which holy men spoke and wrote as it was revealed to them by God.[2] Now, how are we to know whether what we believe is God's truth or man's opinion? By testing it against God's Word. The Bible, being in its original form God's revealed Word to man, speaks the truth for God is Truth. To get to God's doctrine, we have to divide God's Word.

II Timothy 2:15:
Study to shew thyself approved unto God, a workman that needeth not to be ashamed, rightly dividing the word of truth.

We have to study God's Word to know His will. To the extent we rightly divide the Word of Truth, we have true doctrine, that is, right believing and knowledge. When we wrongly divide the Word of Truth, we have false doctrine, man-made doctrine.

Because of the host of different beliefs in Christen-

2. II Timothy 3:16: "All scripture *is* given by inspiration of God, and *is* profitable for doctrine, for reproof, for correction, for instruction in righteousness."

dom taught today, it is evident that not all doctrine is from the rightly-divided Word. Therefore, it is the responsibility of every Christian believer to test to see whether these various doctrines originated in the right or wrong dividing of God's Word.

This book is a summation of my personal quest to test the doctrine of the trinity to see whether it be a man-made or a God-breathed doctrine. The first chapter of this study is a historical look at the evolution of the trinity. This doctrine was nurtured by non-Christian religions and given accreditation by churchmen under political expediency.

is that all?

The second chapter begins the biblical quest. Who is Jesus Christ? Is he God? Or is he the Son of God?

The culminating study is the third chapter, "The Man—Man's Redeemer." Our very redemption, the crucial point on which all of Christianity rests, is dependent on Jesus Christ's being a man and not God. Our passover, which was Jesus Christ tortured, crucified, dead and buried, had to be a sheep from the flock. God would hardly qualify as one of our brethren, yet His Son could.

man, not God

One of the most beautiful and yet illogically interpreted scriptures is the first chapter of the Gospel of John. The final chapter in this book, entitled "Who is the Word" referring to John 1:1, is an intricate study of the first 18 verses of this great revelation.

The book ends with a brief conclusion and five appendixes for a more careful study of certain aspects regarding God, Jesus Christ and the Holy Spirit.

Before closing, let me bare my soul. To say that Jesus Christ is not God in my mind does not degrade the importance and significance of Jesus Christ in any way. It simply elevates God, the Father of our Lord Jesus Christ, to His unique, exalted and unparalleled position. He alone is God.

I do believe the Bible teaches that Jesus Christ is the son of man because he had a human for a mother; and he is the Son of God because of his created conception by God. So on the basis of the parentage of God alone, besides his choosing to live a perfect life, Jesus Christ is by no means a run-of-the-mill, unmarked human being. Thus to say that I do not elevate and respect the position of the Lord Jesus Christ simply because I do not believe the evidence designates Jesus Christ as God is to speak the judgment of a fool, for to the very depth of my being I love him with all my heart, soul, mind and strength.

It is he who sought me out from darkness.

It is he who gave me access to God; even now he is my mediator.

It is he who saved me when I was dead in trespasses and sin.

It is he who gave me the new birth of God's eternal

"created conception by God"

life — which is Christ in me, the hope of glory.

It is he who gave me remission of sins and continues to give forgiveness of sins.

It is he who filled me to capacity by God's presence in Christ in all the fullness of God's gift of holy spirit.

It is he who was made unto me my wisdom, righteousness, sanctification and redemption.

It is he who called me and set me in the heavenlies.

It is he who gave me his joy, peace and love.

It is he who appointed me as a spokesman of God's accurate Word; may I be found faithful in that calling.

It is he who is all in all to me that I might give my all for him.

It is he who is God's only-begotten Son.

May I as a son of God live and die to glorify the God whom men can only know from God's written Word, the Bible, and from the declared Word, God's Son, Jesus Christ.

In spite of all of my human frailties and shortcomings, I endeavor to love him with all my being. I love him and the one and only God who sent him. May His mercy and grace continue to be yours as well as mine, and may God be magnified by our testimony of Him who gave His Son that we might have life and have it more abundantly — yes, that life which is eternal and therefore more than abundant.

CHAPTER ONE

THE ORIGIN OF THE
THREE-IN-ONE GOD

Long before the founding of Christianity the idea of a triune god or a god-in-three persons was a common belief in ancient religions. Although many of these religions had many minor deities, they distinctly acknowledged that there was one supreme God who consisted of three persons or essences. The Babylonians used an equilateral triangle to represent this three-in-one god, now the symbol of the modern three-in-one believers.[1]

The Hindu trinity was made up of the gods Brahma, Vishnu and Shiva. The Greek triad was composed of Zeus, Athena and Apollo. These three were said by the pagans to "agree in one." One of the largest pagan tem-

---

1. Alexander Hislop, *The Two Babylons* (New York: Loizeaux Brothers, 1959), p. 16.

ples built by the Romans was constructed at Baalbek (situated in present-day Lebanon) to their trinity of Jupiter, Mercury and Venus. In Babylon the planet Venus was revered as special and was worshipped as a trinity consisting of Venus, the moon and the sun. This triad became the Babylonian holy trinity in the four-teenth century before Christ.

Not only did non-Christian religions believe in a triune god, but ancient cultures also accepted this idea; cultures such as the Babylonian, Egyptian, Phoenician, Greek, Indian, Chinese, Japanese, Icelandic, Siberian and others.. That the triune concept of God was not only a part of the religions but even permeated the cultures of the dominant ancient nations shows how deeply rooted in human thinking this notion was.

Although other religions for thousands of years before Christ was born worshipped a triune god, the trinity was not a part of Christian dogma and formal documents of the first three centuries after Christ. Certainly, during this time, Church leaders spoke of the Father, Son and Holy Spirit, but they never referred to them as co-equal or of one numerical essence or as three in one. In fact the opposite was the case. They spoke of the Father as supreme, the true and only God, as without beginning, invisible, unbegotten, and as such immutable; and of the Son as inferior, and, as a real person, having a beginning, visible, begotten and mutable.[2]   That there was no formal, established doctrine of the trinity until the fourth century is a fully documented historical fact. The history of the church's first three centuries with regard to the trinity can best be summarized by the concluding paragraph of *The Church of the First Three Centuries* written by Alvan Lamson.

> . . . . The modern doctrine of the Trinity is not found in any document or relic belonging to the Church of the first three centuries. Letters, art, usage, theology, worship, creed, hymn, chant, doxology, ascription, commemorative rite, and festive observance, so far as any remains or any record of them are preserved, coming down from early times, are, as regards this doctrine, an absolute blank. They testify, so far as they testify at all, to the supremacy of the Father, the only true God; and to the inferior and derived nature of the Son. There is nowhere among these remains a co-equal Trinity. The cross is there; Christ is there as the Good Shepherd, the Father's hand placing a crown, or victor's wreath, on his head; but no undivided Three, -- co-equal, infinite, self-existent, and eternal. This was a conception to which the age had not arrived. It was of later origin.[3]

Even such a conservative source as the *New Catholic Encyclopedia* states that trinitarianism became part of Christian doctrine in the fourth, not the first, century.

---

2. Alvan Lamson, *The Church of the First Three Centuries* (Boston: Walker Fuller and Co., 1865), pp. 75, 97, 98.
3. Ibid., p. 396.

It is difficult, in the second half of the 20th century, to offer a clear, objective and straightforward account of the revelation, doctrinal evolution, and theological elaboration of the mystery of the Trinity . . . .

There is . . . recognition on the part of historians of dogma and systematic theologians that when one does speak of an unqualified Trinitarianism, one has moved from the period of Christian origins to, say, the last quadrant of the 4th century. It was only then that what might be called the definitive Trinitarian dogma "one God in three Persons" became thoroughly assimilated into Christian life and thought.

. . . The dogmatic formula "one God in three Persons" . . . was the product of 3 centuries of doctrinal development.[4]

There are, however, evidences of trinitarian concepts being introduced by Christians converted from paganism possibly as early as the last part of the first century. The gradual incorporation of pagan ideologies into Christian doctrine and practice came about by the interaction of four historical components:

1. The early apostles, who had been strong in their knowledge and application of the Word of God, had died. Their steadfastness to God-breathed doctrine was no longer a living example to the followers.
2. The anticipation of the "speedy" return of Christ subsided in the minds of many Christians as time went on.

---

4. *New Catholic Encyclopedia*, 1967, s.v. "Trinity."

3. Many pagans who were converted to Christianity still adhered to some of their previous beliefs and practices. Thus the pure Christian doctrine of the first century was quickly corrupted.

4. Due to the above three elements many people began anticipating a new revival or a new administration to replace the old.[5]

Even while Paul was alive and ministering, the pure gospel which he preached was being contaminated by those who wanted to modify God's Word to their own predilection. Note that the falling away in the Christian Church began to take place shortly after the middle of the first century, toward the end of Paul's ministry.

II Timothy 1:15:
This thou knowest, that all they which are in Asia be turned away from me; of whom are Phygellus and Hermogenes.

II Timothy 4:10:
For Demas hath forsaken me, having loved this present world, and is departed unto Thessalonica; Crescens to Galatia, Titus unto Dalmatia.

Already by the last half of the first century two major sects, other than the adherents to the revelation given to the early apostles, had made in-roads into Christianity. First there were the Ebionites. These were the Judaising Christians who plagued Paul in their at-

---

5. Charles Hase, *A History of the Christian Church* (New York: D. Appleton and Co., 1886), pp. 53-71.

tempt to keep Christian believers under the law and bondage of the Old Testament.[6]   While some of them indeed believed that Jesus was a man born of divine conception, others relegated Jesus to being the son of Joseph and Mary.

Second there were the Gnostics. This sect had its roots in Greek philosophy and religious ideas. They believed that Jesus was a deity, his physical body being either just an appearance or something he borrowed temporarily.[7]

The Apostle John, according to secular sources, was the only apostle to live late in the first century during which time his contributions to the New Testament were written. The true God had the Gospel of John written to clarify Christ's position as the Son of God and the Son of Man (which will be discussed in chapter 3) since sects such as the Ebionites and Gnostics were spreading false doctrines of Christ's position. The Gospel of John establishes the truth of God's Word that Jesus Christ was the Son of God, not "God the Son" or "God Himself."

With the rise of the various sects, the truth of God's Word became infiltrated by idolatrous worship and theories. Christians gradually accepted the foreign elements introduced to their teaching because they were

---

6. Acts 21:20: "And when they heard it, they glorified the Lord, and said unto him, Thou seest, brother, how many thousands of Jews there are which believe; and they are all zealous of the law."
7. Hase, A History of the Christian Church, pp. 53-71.

not being taught the doctrine of God's rightly-divided Word.

To show how quickly some of the foreign elements were introduced to Christianity observe the beginning of the seventh chapter of "The Didache," the anonymous Christian treatise of the late first or early second century. This example of modified doctrine was written sometime between 80 A.D. and 120 A.D.

Κεφ. ζ΄. Περὶ δὲ τοῦ βαπτίσματος, οὕτω βαπτίσατε· ταῦτα πάντα προειπόντες, βαπτίσατε εἰς τὸ ὄνομα τοῦ Πατρὸς καὶ τοῦ Υἱοῦ καὶ τοῦ ἁγίου Πνεύματος ἐν ὕδατι ζῶντι. Ἐὰν δὲ μὴ ἔχῃς ὕδωρ ζῶν, εἰς ἄλλο ὕδωρ βάπτισον· εἰ δ' οὐ δύνασαι ἐν ψυχρῷ, ἐν θερμῷ. Ἐὰν δὲ ἀμφότερα μὴ ἔχῃς, ἔκχεον εἰς τὴν κεφαλὴν τρὶς ὕδωρ εἰς ὄνομα Πατρὸς καὶ Υἱοῦ καὶ ἁγίου Πνεύματος. Πρὸ δὲ τοῦ βαπτίσματος προνηστευσάτω ὁ βαπτίζων καὶ ὁ βαπτιζόμενος καὶ εἴ τινες ἄλλοι δύνανται· κελεύσεις δὲ νηστεῦσαι τὸν βαπτιζόμενον πρὸ μιᾶς ἢ δύο.

Now as regards baptism, thus baptize ye: having first rehearsed all these things, baptize into the name of the Father, and of the Son, and of the Holy Spirit, in running water. But if thou hast not running water, baptize in other water; and if thou canst not in cold, then warm. But if thou hast neither, pour water upon the head thrice, in the name of Father and Son and Holy Spirit. But before the baptism, let the baptizer and the baptized fast, and any others who can; but the baptized thou shalt command to fast for one or two days before. [8]

8. Harry Rimmer, *Crying Stones* (Grand Rapids: Wm. B. Eerdmans Publishing Co., 1946), p. 99.

As early possibly as 80 A.D. this trinitarian baptismal practice was introduced. Baptismal practices of water in the name of Father, the Son and the Holy Ghost replaced the baptism in the name of Jesus Christ.

Clearly, there are two scriptures which in our modern versions of the Bible contain a trinitarian formula. One of these two is found in I John 5.

I John 5:6:
This is he that came by water and blood, *even* Jesus Christ: not by water only, but by water and blood. And it is the Spirit that beareth witness, because the Spirit is truth.

Verse 7:
For there are three that bear record in heaven, the Father, the Word, and the Holy Ghost: and these three are one.

Verse 8:
And there are three that bear witness in earth, the spirit, and the water, and the blood: and these three agree in one.

These verses contain words that do not appear in any of the early manuscripts. The words added begin in verse 7 with "in heaven" and go to "in earth" in verse 8. These words are not found in any of the Greek manuscripts before the sixteenth century. First appearing in Latin copies, the added words crept into the English texts.[9] In other words, all early manuscripts read:

9. *The Companion Bible* (London: The Lamp Press Ltd.), p. 1876.

For there are three that bear record, the spirit, and the water, and the blood: and these three agree in one.

Including more words was an attempt of a scribe or scribes to corrupt the original text with the theology propounded by Irenaeus (second century), Tertullian (early third century; the first person to use the word *trinity* of the Father, Son and Holy Spirit), Cyprian (third century), Hieronymus (fifth century) and Augustine (fifth century).

Since the corruption of I John 5:6-8 had not yet occurred by the fourth century, promoters of trinitarianism and adherents to the trinitarian baptismal formula prior to the fourth century had only one scripture on which to base their new theology and that was Matthew 28:19.

Go ye therefore, and teach all nations, baptizing them in the name of the Father, and of the Son, and of the Holy Ghost.

All extant manuscripts do contain this verse in Matthew 28, the oldest dating from the fourth century during which century trinitarianism was becoming a part of formal doctrine and writing. It would not have been difficult for scribes to insert "in the name of the Father, and of the Son, and of the Holy Ghost," in place of the original "in my name." This must have been what happened because earlier manuscripts from which Eusebius (who died in 340 A.D.) quoted in the early part of the fourth century could not have used the trinitarian words. He cited Matthew 28:19 eighteen times without *once* using them. Rather he wrote, " . . . baptizing them in my name."

The Greek Christian Justin Martyr who wrote in the middle of the second century never quoted "in the name of the Father, and of the Son, and of the Holy Ghost," nor did Aphraates of Nisibis in the early fourth century. This shows that Justin and Aphraates must have had earlier manuscripts than are now in existence.

Furthermore, regarding water baptism, there is no record in the New Testament that the trinitarian baptismal command was ever carried out by the first century Church. They always baptized in the name of Jesus Christ. [10]

Acts 2:38:
Then Peter said unto them. Repent, and be baptized every one of you in the name of Jesus Christ for the remission of sins, and ye shall receive the gift of the Holy Ghost.

Acts 8:16:
(For as yet he was fallen upon none of them: only they were baptized in the name of the Lord Jesus.)

Acts 10:48:
And he commanded them to be baptized in the name of the Lord. Then prayed they him to tarry certain days.

---

10. See V.P. Wierwille, "Baptism," *The Bible Tells Me So* (New Knoxville, Ohio: American Christian Press, 1971).

Acts 19:5:
When they heard *this,* they were baptized in the name of the
Lord Jesus.

It was not difficult for fourth century scribes to
change the words "in my name" to "in the name of the
Father, the Son, and the Holy Ghost" in the few exist-
ing manuscripts, since the Godhead was gradually taking
on a triune nature in their religious environment.

*what about
Syriac?*

Because of doctrinal problems such as baptism presented, reactionary and reforming parties organized to
dissolve the confusion. But the persecution or threat of
persecution of Christians under the Roman emperors
Nero (54-68 A.D.), Domitian (81-96 A.D.), Trajan
(98-117 A.D.) and others simply caused more dissension
within the Christian body.

During the persecution of the second century, a small
group of Christian intellectuals, most prominent of
whom were Aristides and Justin Martyr, wrote discerta-
tions to emperors and other notable persons to defend
the gospel, to stop the persecution and to answer the
charges against them. These dissertations, called Apologies, were, in fact, compromises between Christianity
and paganism. Thus from the apologetic period on, because of the impact the Apologies had, the concepts of
the triune God, plus Mary as the mother of God and
pagan symbolism took root and began growing in discussion and writing.

The attempts at suppressing the early Church by the Roman government ended when Constantine, the Roman emperor, gained power after his victory at the Milvian bridge in 312 A.D. After Constantine's conversion to Christianity he issued an edict at Milan which granted Christians the same rights as the followers of other religions, as well as restitution of wrongs done to Christians.[11] Constantine soon began to grant special favors to Christians which made conversion to Christianity a ticket to political, military and social promotion. So thousands of non-Christians began joining the Church for political favors. In return for granting special favors and acting with leniency, Constantine insisted that he have a strong voice in Church affairs.

It was at Constantine's peak of power, early in the fourth century, that the idea of Jesus Christ's being co-equal with God the Father began to gain a wide base of support. Yet trinitarianism at that point was not an established doctrine. The idea of a triune God stirred great controversy within the Church as there were still many clergy and laymen who did not accept the position of Christ as God.

This disagreement about the position of Christ reached its most noted level in the confrontation between Bishop Alexander of Alexandria, Egypt, and his presbyter Arius. Bishop Alexander taught that Jesus was

---

11. Williston Walker, *A History of the Christian Church,* rev. ed. (New York: Charles Scribner's Sons, 1959), p. 101.

equal to God; Arius did not. So at a synod held at Alexandria in 321, Arius was deposed and excommunicated.[12] Arius, although now in institutional disfavor, still had much support outside of Egypt. Many of the important bishops such as the learned historian, Eusebius of Palestinian Caesarea, and his powerful namesake, Eusebius, Bishop of Nicomedia, theologically agreed with Arius: Jesus Christ is not God.[13]

Constantine, disturbed over the sustained controversy in his empire, sent his ecclesiastical adviser, Ossius, Bishop of Cordova, to Alexandria on a mission of reconciliation and inquiry.[14] After visiting Alexandria, Ossius sided with Alexander against Arius. Ossius returned to Rome and there persuaded Constantine to embrace Alexander's position.[15]

To legitimatize his position, Constantine invited all bishops of the Christian Church to Nicaea (which is now in Asia Minor) in May 325 A.D. Thus, the Council of Nicaea began with its main goal being to settle the dispute over the relationship between God and His Son.

The council consisted of approximately 220 bishops who were almost exclusively from the Occident. Constantine, who was in control of the proceedings, used his political power to bring pressure to bear on the bishops

12. Hase, *A History of the Christian Church*, p. 111.
13. Henry Chadwick, *The Early Church* (Grand Rapids: Wm. B. Eerdmans Publishing Co., 1968), p. 129.
14. Ibid.
15. Ibid., p. 130.

to accept his theological position. The creed they signed was clearly anti-Arian; in other words, the Nicene Creed embraced the Son as co-equal with God. Two hundred eighteen of the 220 bishops signed this creed, although it was truly the work of a minority. [16]

The *Encyclopedia Britannica* summarizes the proceedings of the Council of Nicaea as follows:

The Council of Nicaea met on May 20, 325. Constantine himself presiding, actively guiding the discussion, and personally proposed (no doubt on Ossius' prompting) the crucial formula expressing the relation of Christ to God in the creed issued by the council, "of one substance with the Father." Over-awed by the emperor, the bishops, with two exceptions only, signed the creed, many of them against their inclination.

Constantine regarded the decision of Nicaea as divinely inspired. As long as he lived no one dared openly to challenge the Creed of Nicaea, but the expected concord did not follow. [17]

Although the Nicene Creed had been accepted by the council of bishops, there still remained great dissension among many of the clergy about the deity of Jesus Christ. So in the year 381 A.D. a second ecumenical

16. Henry Bettenson, ed., *Documents of the Christian Church*, 2nd ed. (London: Oxford University Press, 1963), p. 58. "Arius and his followers were forthwith banished to Illyria and his works were burned. The reverberations of this treatment of Arius had a profound effect on the Church, as well as on Constantine, for several decades. Just as Arius was to have been pardoned by Constantine and reinstated in the Church, he died."
17. *Encyclopedia Britannica*, 1968, s.v. "Council of Nicaea."

council met in Constantinople.[18] This council reaffirmed the Nicene Creed stating that Jesus and God were co-equal and co-eternal, and also declared the deity of the Holy Spirit. The doctrine of the trinity was then fully established and thus became the cornerstone of Christian faith for the next fifteen centuries.[19]

Clearly, historians of Church dogma and systematic theologians agree that the idea of a Christian trinity was not a part of the first century Church. The twelve apostles never subscribed to it or received revelation about it. So how then did a trinitarian doctrine come about? It gradually evolved and gained momentum in late first, second and third centuries as pagans, who had converted to Christianity, brought to Christianity some of their pagan beliefs and practices. Trinitarianism then

---

18. B. K. Kuiper, *The Church in History* (Grand Rapids: Wm. B. Eerdmans Publishing Co., 1951), p. 128.

19. The Nicene Creed: "We believe in one God the Father all sovereign, maker of heaven and earth, and of all things visible and invisible:

And in one Lord Jesus Christ, the only-begotten Son of God, Begotten of the Father before all the ages, Light of Light, true God of true God, begotten not made, of one substance with the Father, through whom all things were made; who for us men and for our salvation came down from the heavens, and was made flesh of the Holy Spirit and the Virgin Mary, and became man, and was crucified for us under Pontius Pilate, and suffered and was buried, and rose again on the third day according to the Scriptures, and ascended into the heavens, and sitteth on the right hand of the Father, and cometh again with glory to judge living and dead, of whose kingdom there shall be no end:

And in the Holy Spirit, the Lord and the Life-giver, that proceedeth from the Father, who with Father and Son is worshipped together and glorified together, who spake through the prophets:

In one holy Catholic and Apostolic Church:

We acknowledge one baptism unto remission of sins. We look for a resurrection of the dead, and the life of the age to come."

was confirmed at Nicaea in 325 by Church bishops out of political expediency. Its reaffirmation was thereafter needed and received at Constantinople in 381. Since that time the "God-in-three-persons" doctrine has been adhered to as though it were divine revelation. The following chapters of this book will show that it is not.

CHAPTER TWO

WHO IS JESUS CHRIST?

In the Bible the phrase *Son of God*, referring to Jesus Christ, is found 50 times. At no place is there *God the Son*. Without "God the Son," Jesus Christ cannot be God.

The well-defined difference between God and the Son of God can be seen most clearly from a comprehensive study of God's Word while applying the biblical principles of interpretation. These are absolutely foundational to an accurate knowledge of God's Word. The lack of understanding and application of these primary principles has contributed to the misconceptions of the significance of Jesus Christ, the Son of God.

One of these principles is that *things similar are not identical.* For example, let's say there are two men who look alike, they could both be clergymen, also vocalists, and even periodically mistaken for one another. Yet they are two different people. Similarities are not identities. Two paintings could be similar in every respect, yet they are not the selfsame. An art collector is readily aware of this. Likewise, counterfeit money is not real money, no matter how close the similarity.

Jesus Christ is similar to God in many aspects, but Jesus Christ and God are not identical. They are not one and the same; they are not co-equal. Who then is Jesus Christ? To answer this question, let's go back to the beginning.

Where was Jesus Christ before he was born to Mary? Jesus Christ was with God in His foreknowledge. The first epistle of Peter makes this clear.

I Peter 1:20:
Who [Christ] verily was foreordained [Carefully note this word "foreordained" in its context.] before the foundation of the world, but was manifest in these last times for you.

The word "foreordained" is the Greek word *proginōskō* which means "to foreknow." God foreknew Christ; Christ was in God's foreknowledge before the foundation of the world, but Christ was manifested when he was born.

The same Greek word which is translated "foreordained" in this verse, I Peter 1:20, is translated "foreknow" in Romans 8.

Romans 8:29:
For whom he did foreknow, he also did predestinate ....

Jesus Christ was with God before the foundation of the world, meaning that God foreknew him. Since Jesus Christ was with God before the foundation of the world, then by the usage of this word "foreknow" which is the same as "foreordain," we, the believers, were also with God in the beginning. Ephesians 1 tells this.

Ephesians 1:4:
According as he [God] hath chosen us in him [God] before the foundation of the world, that we should be holy and without blame before him [God] in love.

We, as well as Jesus Christ, were with God in His foreknowledge, but not in existence, before the foundation of the world.

Both Jesus Christ and we believers were known of God before the foundation of the world because God is omniscient. God knew that Adam would fall and that man would need a legal redeemer.

II Timothy 1:9:
Who [God] hath saved us, and called *us* with an holy calling, not according to our works, but according to his own purpose and grace, which was given us in Christ Jesus before the world began.

We did not exist before the world began. Neither did Jesus Christ. However, in God's foreknowledge, redemption was a reality since God foreknew that the deeds of Adam would be followed by the accomplishments of Jesus Christ. Jesus Christ was with God (in His foreknowledge) before the foundation of the world. Jesus Christ did not exist. This dissimilarity alone proves that God and the Son of God are not an identity.

After seeing that similarities are not identities, a second principle of interpretation must be applied in researching the topic at hand. This principle is that *when there are an abundance of clear scriptures regarding an identical situation or person and only a few apparently contradicting scriptures, the many clear ones must not be subordinated or rationalized while the few are exclusively adhered to or allowed to dominate; but rather the few must fit with the many.* In applying this principle, we note that Jesus Christ is directly referred to as the "Son of God" in more than 50 verses in the New Testament; he is called "God" in four. (Never is he called "God the Son.") By sheer weight of this evidence alone, 50 to 4, the truth should be evident. But let's delve into the four exceptions anyway in order to see them in harmony with the more than 50 verses.

I Timothy 3 contains one of these four times when the word "God" is used referring to Jesus Christ.

I Timothy 3:16:
And without controversy great is the mystery of godliness:
God [meaning Jesus Christ] was manifest in the flesh, justified
in the Spirit, seen of angels, preached unto the Gentiles,
believed on in the world, received up into glory.

The word "God" in the above verse is in Greek the
relative pronoun *hos*, meaning "which." *Hos* is found in
all Critical Greek texts except Stephens, the text used
for the King James translation. How the error using
"God" instead of "which" crept into Stephens is easy to
perceive. The relative pronoun "which" looks similar in
Greek to our two English letters "OC." However, by
putting a small horizontal line in the "Θ" and a line over
the top of the two letters $\overline{\Theta C}$, they produce the abbrevi-
ation for God found in the Greek uncials.[1] The original
text probably read *ho* rather than *hos*.

And without controversy great is the mystery of godliness
which [Jesus Christ] was manifest in the flesh ....

The word "God" could not have been in the original
manuscripts. By using the original word "which," there

1. On page 1803 in the Companion Bible, the following is stated: "The
R.V. prints 'He who,' and adds in margin, '*Theos* (God) rests on no
sufficient evidence.' The probability is that the original reading was *ho*
(which), with the Syriac and all the Latin Versions, to agree with
mustērion (neut.). The Greek uncial being O, some scribe added the letter
"s", making $\overline{OC}$ (He who), which he thought made better sense. Later
another put a mark, in this Θ, making the word $\overline{\Theta C}$, the contraction for
THEOS, God. This mark in Codex A, in the British Museum, is said by
some to be in different ink." The Codex Claromontams, Uncial 061,
the Vulgate and some old Latin manuscripts contain *ho* rather than *hos*.

remains no contradiction between this and the 50 clear verses about the Son of God.

Another scripture using the word "God" when referring to Jesus Christ is Hebrews 1:8.

Hebrews 1:8:
But unto the Son *he saith,* Thy throne, O God, *is* for ever and ever: a sceptre of righteousness *is* the sceptre of thy kingdom.

This is apparently a quotation from Psalms 45:6 where the word "God" refers to a man, a man in an exalted position, namely, the king.

The first three chapters of Hebrews contain a discussion of Christ in the variety of roles he had and the titles he was given; for example, "the brightness of his glory" (1:3); "being made so much better than the angels" (1:4); "the Apostle and High Priest of our profession" (3:1). Every verse leading up to verse 8 in Hebrews 1 emphasizes the greatness of Christ and what he did; thus the title of "God." It is only a formal title, used here to indicate his power and glory.

Calling a person "God" is not that unique in Oriental usage. In the Bible there are three other specific instances when the word "God" is used of a person. Jehovah called Moses a "god."

Exodus 7:1:
And the Lord said unto Moses, See, I have made thee a god to Pharaoh: and Aaron thy brother shall be thy prophet.

The judges of Israel, in very common usage, were referred to as gods.

Exodus 22:28:
Thou shalt not revile the gods [the judges], nor curse the ruler of thy people.

The children of the most high are also referred to as gods.

Psalms 82:6:
I have said, Ye *are* gods; and all of you *are* children of the most High.

Two verses later in the same psalm it is told that the responsible leader is to judge the earth; he is also called god.

Psalms 82:8:
Arise, O God, judge the earth: for thou shalt inherit all nations.

Still practiced in parts of the East today a king's subjects and servants would address him, the king, as the "lord" or as the "lord and god." A wife speaking of her husband would address him in like manner. An example of this Oriental custom is found in the Old Testament when Ruth addressed her husband Boaz as her lord.

Ruth 2:13:
Then she said, Let me find favour in thy sight, my lord; for that thou hast comforted me, and for that thou hast spoken friendly unto thine handmaid, though I be not like unto one of thine handmaidens.

The Hebrew word for "lord" is *adon*, meaning "headship" and "god as over-lord." Thus the usage of God in Hebrews 1:8 shows Jesus Christ in an exalted position; he is, however, not God the Creator.

The third instance of Jesus Christ's being referred to as God is done so by the Apostle Thomas when he first sees the resurrected Christ.

John 20:28:
And Thomas answered and said unto him, My Lord and my God.

This scripture is a natural follow-up of Hebrews 1:8 where Thomas acknowledged Jesus Christ in an exalted position by placing himself in lower status. "My Lord and my God" pays greatest homage to the resurrected one.

However, an even greater truth is shown by the usage of Thomas' addressing Jesus Christ as "my Lord and my God." It brings to light the precision of a figure of speech. The specific figure of speech is called *hendiadys*. Literally, the figure *hendiadys* means "one by means of two." Whenever two words are used but only one idea intended, it is the figure *hendiadys.* One of the two words expresses the fact and the other intensifies it to the superlative degree, thus making the statement especially emphatic. This method gives considerable cogency to an expression. When Thomas exclaimed "My Lord and my God," he was observing the resurrected Christ as "my godly Lord." The word "lord" expresses the fact and the word "godly" intensifies "lord" to the superlative degree. Indeed my godly Lord is exactly what Jesus Christ is!

The fourth apparently thorny scripture is the familiar verse from Isaiah 9.

Isaiah 9:6:
For unto us a child is born, unto us a son is given: and the government shall be upon his shoulder: and his name shall be called Wonderful, Counseller, The mighty God, The everlasting Father, The Prince of Peace.

The words "Jesus Christ" are not specifically used in this scripture; however, many people believe it is a prophecy referring to him. If indeed this is the case, then the following facts apply: the quotation saying, "His name shall be called," means that this is the definition of his name.

The Massoretic text of Isaiah 9:6 reads, "Wonderful in counsel is God the mighty, the everlasting Father, the ruler of peace." The Septuagint reads, "For a child is born to us, and a son is given to us, whose government is

upon his shoulder: and his name is called the messenger
of great counsel: for I will bring peace upon the princes,
and health to him."

"And his name shall be called . . . " is simply another
example of the meaning of a name, such as *Jacob* means
"supplanter" and *Sarah* means "princess." So if this
prophecy in Isaiah 9:6 does refer to Jesus Christ, it
simply tells us that his name means "Wonderful, Counseller, the mighty God, The everlasting Father, The
Prince of Peace," and it does not make him any of these
things, including "the mighty God."

Having examined the four scriptures commonly used in
showing that Jesus Christ is God because they appeared
to do so, let us now take a look at some of the 50
clear scripture verses as well as many others which dis-
tinguish Christ as the Son of God.

Have you ever asked why various scriptures were
recorded? The express purpose for the Word of God
regarding Jesus Christ is that men may know that he is
not God the Creator, but the Son of God.

John 20:31:
But these are written, that ye might believe that Jesus is the
Christ, the Son of God; and that believing ye might have life
through his name.

The Scriptures were written not that we might believe
that Jesus is God, but rather that we might believe that
he is the Son of God.

According to the Word of God, God said Jesus Christ was His Son. Here are the other witnesses who proclaimed the same: John the Baptist, all the gospel writers (Matthew, Mark, Luke and John), Simon Peter, Nathanael, the centurion, God's angels, the blind man, Martha, Philip and the Ethiopian eunuch (a palace official), Paul, the revilers and mockers at the cross, devil spirits, the high priest Caiaphas, disciples in the boat on Galilee, elders of the people, and others — including Jesus Christ himself.

In examining the witnesses, let's look first of all at what God the Creator said about Jesus Christ.

Matthew 3:17:
And lo a voice from heaven, saying, This is my beloved Son, in whom I am well pleased.

Matthew 17:5:
While he yet spake, behold, a bright cloud overshadowed them: and behold a voice out of the cloud, which said, This is my beloved Son, in whom I am well pleased; hear ye him.

Mark 1:11:
And there came a voice from heaven, *saying,* Thou art my beloved Son, in whom I am well pleased.

Mark 9:7:
And there was a cloud that overshadowed them: and a voice came out of the cloud, saying, This is my beloved Son: hear him.

Luke 9:35:
And there came a voice out of the cloud, saying, This is my beloved Son: hear him.

Mark made it known that he believed Jesus Christ to be the Son of God, not God.

Mark 1:1:
The beginning of the gospel of Jesus Christ, the Son of God.

John made it known that he believed Jesus Christ to be the Son of God, not God.

John 1:18:
No man hath seen God at any time; the only begotten Son, which is in the bosom of the Father, he hath declared *him.*

John 20:31:
But these are written, that ye might believe that Jesus is the Christ, the Son of God; and that believing ye might have life through his name.

I John 1:3:
That which we have seen and heard declare we unto you, that ye also may have fellowship with us; and truly our fellowship *is* with the Father, and with his Son Jesus Christ.

I John 4:15:
Whosoever shall confess that Jesus is the Son of God, God dwelleth in him, and he in God.

I John 5:5:
Who is he that overcometh the world, but he that believeth that Jesus is the Son of God?

I John 5:20:
And we know that the Son of God is come, and hath given us an understanding, that we may know him that is true, and we are in him that is true, *even* in his Son Jesus Christ. This is the true God, and eternal life.

II John 3:
Grace be with you, mercy, *and* peace, from God the Father, and from the Lord Jesus Christ, the Son of the Father, in truth and love.

Paul made it known that he believed Jesus Christ to be the Son of God, not God.

Acts 9:20:
And straightway he preached Christ in the synagogues, that he is the Son of God.

Romans 1:3 and 4:
Concerning his Son Jesus Christ our Lord, which was made of the seed of David according to the flesh;

And declared *to be* the Son of God with power, according to the spirit of holiness, by the resurrection from the dead.

Romans 5:10:
For if, when we were enemies, we were reconciled to God by

the death of his Son, much more, being reconciled, we shall be saved by his life.

Romans 8:3:
For what the law could not do, in that it was weak through the flesh, God sending his own Son in the likeness of sinful flesh, and for sin, condemned sin in the flesh.

I Corinthians 1:9:
God *is* faithful, by whom ye were called unto the fellowship of his Son Jesus Christ our Lord.

II Corinthians 1:19:
For the Son of God, Jesus Christ, who was preached among you by us, *even* by me and Silvanus and Timotheus, was not yea and nay, but in him was yea.

Galatians 2:20:
I am crucified with Christ: nevertheless I live; yet not I, but Christ liveth in me: and the life which I now live in the flesh I live by the faith of the Son of God, who loved me, and gave himself for me.

Galatians 4:4:
But when the fulness of the time was come, God sent forth his Son, made of a woman, made under the law.

God's angel knew that Jesus Christ was the Son of God, not God.

Luke 1:35:
And the angel answered and said unto her, The Holy Ghost

shall come upon thee, and the power of the Highest shall overshadow thee: therefore also that holy thing which shall be born of thee shall be called the Son of God.

John the Baptist made it known that he believed Jesus Christ to be the Son of God, not God.

John 1:32-34:
And John bare record, saying, I saw the Spirit descending from heaven like a dove, and it abode upon him.

And I knew him not: but he that sent me to baptize with water, the same said unto me, Upon whom thou shalt see the Spirit descending, and remaining on him, the same is he which baptizeth with the Holy Ghost.

And I saw, and bare record that this is the Son of God.

Simon Peter made it known that he believed Jesus Christ to be the Son of God, not God.

Matthew 16:16:
And Simon Peter answered and said, Thou art the Christ, the Son of the living God.

John 6:68 and 69:
Then Simon Peter answered him, Lord, to whom shall we go? thou hast the words of eternal life.

And we believe and are sure that thou art that Christ, the Son of the living God.

Nathanael made it known that he believed Jesus Christ to be the Son of God, not God.

John 1:49:
Nathanael answered and saith unto him, Rabbi, thou art the Son of God; thou art the King of Israel.

Martha made it known that she believed Jesus Christ to be the Son of God, not God.

John 11:27:
She saith unto him, Yea, Lord: I believe thou art the Christ, the Son of God, which should come into the world.

The man who was born blind made it known that he believed Jesus Christ to be the Son of God, not God.

John 9:35-38:
Jesus heard that they had cast him out; and when he had found him, he said unto him, Dost thou believe on the Son of God?

He answered and said, Who is he, Lord, that I might believe on him?

And Jesus said unto him, Thou hast both seen him, and it is he that talketh with thee.

And he said, Lord, I believe. And he worshipped him.

The man born blind called Jesus Christ "lord" even

before he knew Jesus Christ to be the Son of God. The man naturally recognized Jesus Christ as his superior. The man "worshipped him," according to verse 38, not because he was God the Creator but because he was a religious man superior to himself who had done him a miraculous service.

The disciples in the ship made it known that they believed Jesus Christ to be the Son of God, not God.

Matthew 14:33:
Then they that were in the ship came and worshipped him, saying, Of a truth thou art the Son of God.

Philip and the Ethiopian eunuch believed Jesus Christ to be the Son of God, not God.

Acts 8:37:
And Philip said, If thou believest with all thine heart, thou mayest. And he answered and said, I believe that Jesus Christ is the Son of God.

The centurion and others made it known that they believed Jesus Christ to be the Son of God, not God.

Matthew 27:54:
Now when the centurion, and they that were with him, watching Jesus, saw the earthquake, and those things that were done, they feared greatly, saying, Truly this was the Son of God.

Devil spirits made it known that they believed Jesus Christ to be the Son of God, not God.

Matthew 8:29:
And, behold, they cried out, saying, What have we to do with thee, Jesus, thou Son of God? art thou come hither to torment us before the time?

Mark 3:11:
And unclean spirits, when they saw him, fell down before him, and cried, saying, Thou art the Son of God.

Mark 5:7:
And [the devil spirits] cried with a loud voice, and said, What have I to do with thee, Jesus, *thou* Son of the most high God? I adjure thee by God, that thou torment me not.

Luke 4:41:
And devils also came out of many, crying out, and saying, Thou art Christ the Son of God. And he rebuking them suffered *them* not to speak: for they knew that he was Christ.

Luke 8:28:
When he saw Jesus, he cried out, and fell down before him, and with a loud voice said, What have I to do with thee, Jesus, *thou* Son of God most high? I beseech thee, torment me not.

Jesus Christ made it known that he believed himself to be the Son of God, not God. And he should have known.

Matthew 27:43:
He trusted in God; let him deliver him now, if he will have him: for he said, I am the Son of God.

John 3:16-18:
For God so loved the world, that he gave his only begotten Son, that whosoever believeth in him should not perish, but have everlasting life.

For God sent not his Son into the world to condemn the world; but that the world through him might be saved.

He that believeth on him is not condemned: but he that believeth not is condemned already, because he hath not believed in the name of the only begotten Son of God.

John 5:25:
Verily, verily, I say unto you, The hour is coming, and now is, when the dead shall hear the voice of the Son of God: and they that hear shall live.

John 9:35,37:
Jesus heard that they had cast him out; and when he had found him, he said unto him, Dost thou believe on the Son of God?

And Jesus said unto him, Thou hast both seen him, and it is he that talketh with thee.

John 10:36:
Say ye of him, whom the Father hath sanctified, and sent into the world, Thou blasphemest; because I said, I am the Son of God?

The above scriptures record some of the important witnesses who believed Jesus to be the Son of God. Certainly vast and varied persons attested to that fact.

Earlier we noted that similarities do not prove identity. In fact, according to all laws of logic, one point of dissimilarity *disproves* identity. There are numerous positions on which Jesus Christ and God are dissimilar. One of these differences pertains to temptation.

James 1:13:
Let no man say when he is tempted, I am tempted of God: for God cannot be tempted with evil, neither tempteth he any man.

God cannot be tempted, yet Jesus Christ was in all points tempted.

Luke 4:1,2,13:
And Jesus being full of the Holy Ghost returned from Jordan, and was led by the Spirit into the wilderness,

Being forty days tempted of the devil . . . .

And when the devil had ended all the temptation, he departed from him for a season.

Hebrews 4:15:
For we have not an high priest which cannot be touched with the feeling of our infirmities; but was in all points tempted like as *we are, yet* without sin.

Jesus Christ was tempted in all points as we are, yet God is never tempted; indeed, cannot be tempted.

Another difference between God and Jesus Christ regards that of knowledge. God is omniscient, but Jesus Christ knew only those things which he ascertained from his knowledge of the Scriptures and from the rest of the senses world, plus that which God revealed to him.

Mark 13:32:
But of that day and *that* hour knoweth no man, no, not the angels which are in heaven, neither the Son, but the Father.

This clearly shows the limitations of Jesus Christ's knowledge.

Besides this difference in knowledge between God and Jesus Christ, the Scriptures also indicate that God's will is a separate and distinct will from Jesus Christ's.

Matthew 26:39:
And he went a little farther, and fell on his face, and prayed, saying, O my Father, if it be possible, let this cup pass from me: nevertheless not as I will, but as thou *wilt*.

Matthew 26:42:
He went away again the second time, and prayed, saying, O my Father, if this cup may not pass away from me, except I drink it, thy will be done.

Luke 22:42:
Saying, Father, if thou be willing, remove this cup from me: nevertheless not my will, but thine, be done.

John 5:30:
I can of mine own self do nothing: as I hear, I judge: and my judgment is just; because I seek not mine own will, but the will of the Father which hath sent me.

Matthew 20:23:
And he saith unto them, Ye shall drink indeed of my cup, and be baptized with the baptism that I am baptized with: but to sit on my right hand, and on my left, is not mine to give, but *it shall be given to them* for whom it is prepared of my Father.

What about when Jesus say He + Fath one World perso

These five citations demonstrate that Jesus Christ carried out his Father's will while putting his own wishes aside. The Scriptures also make a distinction between Jesus Christ who was a man and God who is Spirit.

note parallel texts

Matthew 12:32:
And whosoever speaketh a word against the Son of man, it shall be forgiven him: but whosoever speaketh against the Holy Ghost, it shall not be forgiven him, neither in this world, neither in the *world* to come.

John 7 shows Jesus Christ as accepting God's doctrine, a doctrine which didn't originate in Jesus Christ's mind.

John 7:16:
Jesus answered them, and said, My doctrine is not mine, but his that sent me.

John 8 points out that Jesus Christ and God are clearly two, not one.

John 8:17 and 18:
It is also written in your law, that the testimony of two men is true.

I am one that bear witness of myself, and the Father that sent me beareth witness of me.

Even today, at this time, Jesus Christ is not God;[2] he is in the heavenlies at the right hand of God.

Mark 14:62:
And Jesus said, I am: and ye shall see the Son of man sitting on the right hand of power, and coming in the clouds of heaven.

Mark 16:19:
So then after the Lord had spoken unto them, he was received up into heaven, and sat on the right hand of God.

Acts 7:55:
But he, being full of the Holy Ghost, looked up stedfastly into heaven, and saw the glory of God, and Jesus standing on the right hand of God.

---

2. Jesus Christ doesn't change. Hebrews 13:8 says, "Jesus Christ the same yesterday, and to day, and for ever."

Hebrews 1:3:
Who being the brightness of *his* glory, and the express image of his person, and upholding all things by the word of his power, when he had by himself purged our sins, sat down on the right hand of the Majesty on high.

The scriptures which say that Jesus Christ and his Father are one do not indicate that Jesus Christ was God, but rather that Jesus Christ and God had unity of purpose, they worked in a unified effort. These same scriptures also specify that we can be one with them — not that we become God, but that we have a unity of purpose with God and His Son, Jesus Christ.

John 10:30:
I and *my* Father are one.

"One" is the Greek word *hen,* neuter, meaning one in purpose, not one person which would be *heis,* masculine. This is the climax of Jesus' claim of oneness with the Father, and this oneness is of purpose.

John 17:11:
And now I am no more in the world, but these [disciples] are in the world, and I come to thee. Holy Father, keep through thine own name those whom thou hast given me, that they may be one, as we *are.*

John 17:20-23:
Neither pray I for these alone, but for them also which shall believe on me through their word;

That they all may be one; as thou, Father, *art* in me, and I in thee, that they also may be one in us: that the world may believe that thou hast sent me.

And the glory which thou gavest me I have given them; that they may be one, even as we are one:

I in them, and thou in me, that they may be made perfect in one; and that the world may know that thou hast sent me, and hast loved them, as thou hast loved me.

The word "one" does not mean "equal to," but rather signifies "unity of purpose." When you and I are one, we have unity of purpose pertaining to the matters in which we're mutually involved.

John 14:28 and I Corinthians 11:3 boldly indicate that God is superior to Jesus Christ.

John 14:28:
Ye have heard how I said unto you, I go away, and come *again* unto you. If ye loved me, ye would rejoice, because I said, I go unto the Father: for my Father is greater than I.

I Corinthians 11:3:
But I would have you know, that the head of every man is Christ; and the head of the woman *is* the man; and the head of Christ *is* God.

In this same context, Philippians 2:6 poses an interesting question.

Who, being in the form of God, thought it not robbery to be equal with God.

How can Jesus Christ be equal with God and yet, according to other scriptures, God be superior to Jesus Christ?

The word "equal" in Philippians 2:6 is the Greek word *isos* from which is derived the English word "isosceles." An isosceles triangle has two angles which contain the exact same number of degrees. Even though equal, the angles are not identical.

Besides this, the equality of Philippians 2:6 hinges on our understanding of Oriental mannerisms. The Jews brought this to light in John 5:18.

John 5:18:
Therefore the Jews sought the more to kill him [Jesus Christ], because he not only had broken the sabbath, but said also that God was his Father, making himself equal with God.[3]

Thus, according to Oriental culture, a son is equal to his father. When Jesus Christ said that God was his Father, he put himself on par with God. It did not make him God, but it gave him many of the same privileges as

---

3. The Jews never even considered the possibility of Jesus' being God. They knew the Messiah would not be God, thus a man claiming to be God wouldn't have agitated them for they would have recognized such a person as being mentally ill. But a person's claiming to be the Son of God was disturbing because according to Judaic doctrine that was a possibility. They simply rejected Jesus as that promised Messiah.

God. Similarly, a son born into the family of a king has many of the same basic privileges as his father, but yet the king represents the greater of the two. The father is always greater than the son, but yet their privileges are many times equal because of the father's power and position to make them so.

Furthermore, in verse 5 of Philippians 2, God exhorts us: "Let this mind be in you which was also in Christ Jesus." Then verse 6 says that Jesus Christ thought it not robbery to be equal with God. If we let these same thoughts be in us that Jesus Christ had, then we bring ourselves up to that level of equality as sons of God. What a tremendous lever for the more than abundant life if we put on the thoughts of Christ.

Verses 7 through 11 of Philippians 2 further explain that Jesus Christ humbled himself and, as a result, God highly exalted him.

Philippians 2:7-11:
But made himself of no reputation, and took upon him the form of a servant, and was made in the likeness of men:

And being found in fashion as a man, he humbled himself, and became obedient unto death, even the death of the cross.

Wherefore God also hath highly exalted him, and given him a name which is above every name:

[Why did God exalt Jesus and give him a name which is above every name?] That at the name of Jesus every knee should bow, of *things* in heaven, and *things* in earth, and *things* under the earth;

And *that* every tongue should confess that Jesus Christ *is* Lord, to the glory of God the Father.

So when we confess that Jesus Christ is our Lord, it gives glory to God the Father of our Lord Jesus Christ.

It was Jesus Christ, the Son of God, who made it possible for us also to be sons of God, not after the flesh but after the spirit.

I Corinthians 8:6:
But to us *there is but* one God, the Father, of whom *are* all things, and we in him; and one Lord Jesus Christ, by whom *are* all things, and we by him.

NOT EXPLAINED

I John 3:2:
Beloved, now are we the sons of God . . . .

What did Jesus Christ, the only-begotten, do to accomplish sonship for us? Hebrews 2 explains this so completely.

Hebrews 2:9-11:
But we see Jesus, who was made a little lower than the angels [God] [4] for the suffering of death, crowned with glory and honour; that he by the grace of God should taste death for every man.

TEXT

---

4. This entire phrase is a quote from Psalms 8:5. The word translated "angels" is the Hebrew word *Elohim*, God.

For it became him, for whom *are* all things, and by whom *are* all things, in bringing many sons unto glory, to make the captain of their salvation perfect through sufferings.

For both he that sanctifieth and they who are sanctified *are* all of one [God]: for which cause he is not ashamed to call them brethren.

Since we are sons of God and Jesus Christ is the Son of God, we are, as it says in Hebrews, his brothers. Being brothers of Jesus Christ, we now are on legal par with him. Jesus Christ was not and is not God, neither are we; but we are heirs of God and joint-heirs with Christ. Furthermore Jesus Christ is also our redeemer and our lord. He is *the* Son of God. We could say if questioned by Jesus as his disciples were, "But whom say ye that I am?"

Thou art the Christ, the Son of the living God.

CHAPTER THREE

THE MAN — MAN'S REDEEMER

F ollowing upon the Ten Commandments in Deuteronomy 5, there is stated in Deuteronomy 6 a reiteration of the greatest truth of the supremacy of the one God.

Deuteronomy 6:4:
Hear, O Israel: The Lord [*Jehovah*] our God [*Elohim*] *is* one Lord [*Jehovah*].

Elohim is used of God as the Creator; *Jehovah* is used of God in relationship to His creation. "The *Jehovah* our *Elohim* is one *Jehovah*," and He is the one and only one.

There has always been one sin which God did not and will not tolerate and that is worshipping any god other than God the Creator. When we defy the basic rule God set up in the very beginning, serving gods other

LOOK WHAT HE IS SAYING TO CENTURIES OF Xns!

than the one true God, we bring injury to ourselves. Then we make matters even worse, after disregarding God's will in our own lives, by propounding it to others.

Jesus Christ is not God. Biblically he is the Son of God. This in no way detracts from the uniqueness of Christ. His position is second only to God, being God's "only-begotten Son."

God in His foreknowledge knew that Adam would transfer his God-given rights to Satan and then that He, God, would have to beget a Son to redeem man; therefore, in the very beginning He formed, made and created man in such a manner that man's redemption could be made on legal grounds. To fathom how a redeemer, the Messiah, could retrieve man from the power of Satan, we will first endeavor to understand the manner in which God formed, made and created man so that mankind would be legally redeemable.

To understand the origin of man, a scripture in Isaiah must be rightly divided.

Isaiah 43:7:
Even every one that is called by my name: for I have created him for my glory, I have formed him; yea, I have made him.

God said He *created* man for His glory; He *formed* him and *made* him. Are the three words "created," "formed" and "made" synonymous? If God's Word means what it says and says what it means, these words cannot be synonymous, otherwise words are useless as a means of communication. When God said "formed," He meant formed. When He said "made," He meant made. When He said "created," He meant created. Had God meant "formed" throughout, it would have said "formed" at all three places. But God said, "I created, formed and made man."

In I Thessalonians, God uses three other words to define the man He created, formed and made for His glory.

I Thessalonians 5:23:
And the very God of peace sanctify you wholly; and *I pray God* your whole spirit and soul and body be preserved blameless unto the coming of our Lord Jesus Christ.

Are these three words "spirit," "soul" and "body" synonymous? No more so than "created," "formed" and "made" are synonymous. "Body" means body, "soul" means soul, and "spirit" means spirit. Man consisted of three parts; one part God formed, one He made and one He created. The Word of God speaks for itself regarding what was formed, what was made and what was created, as well as what is body, soul and spirit. Let us follow the disclosure of scriptures.

Genesis 2:7:
And the Lord God formed man *of* the dust of the ground ....

The Hebrew word for "formed" is *yatsar* "to fashion from something that is already in existence." Genesis 2:7 says that God formed man of the dust of the ground, a substance which existed before God fashioned man's body. Man's body is composed of the same elements that are in the dust of the earth.

Genesis 3:19:
In the sweat of thy face shalt thou eat bread, till thou return unto the ground; for out of it wast thou taken: for dust thou *art*, and unto dust shalt thou return.

The body of man was formed, *yatsar*, of the dust of the ground. And, because of the natural law that everything must ultimately return to its original state, the body must return to dust. Ecclesiastes 3:20 says, ". . . All are of the dust, and all return to dust again." This obviously refers to the body of man.

The next word to observe is the word "soul" which in Hebrew is *nephesh*. What is soul? The soul in man is that which gives the body its life, its vitality.

Genesis 2:7:
And the Lord God formed man (man's body) *of* the dust of the ground, and breathed into his nostrils the breath of life; and man became a living soul.

The soul, *nephesh*, of man is the part God made, *asah,* by breathing into his formed body the breath of life.

God put life into Adam; He *made* man a living *soul*.
The word "made" means "a substance required of which
the thing made consists." The soul is nothing more or
less than that which gives life to a person's body. Some-
times it is called "the spirit of man." Soul has nothing
to do with whether you are a Christian or a non-Christian. So long as a person breathes, he has soul.

Acts 27:37:
And we were in all in the ship two hundred threescore and
sixteen souls.

This record in Acts refers to the ship on which Paul
and Luke were sailing to Rome. Except for Paul, Luke
and Aristarchus, the rest on board were unbelievers,
non-Christians; and yet the record says, "and we were in
all in the ship two hundred threescore and sixteen
souls." In other words there were 276 alive people on
Paul's ship. If a body is alive it has soul.

The confusion between the soul and the spirit has
caused no end of difficulty for people. Some people
say the soul is immortal, for instance. They talk of
transmigration of the soul, the immortality of the soul.
These are all erroneous usages of words concerning
subjects which are set with exactness and precision in
the Word of God.

Genesis 1:30:
And to every beast of the earth, and to every fowl of the air,
and to every thing that creepeth upon the earth, wherein *there
is* life ...

The word "life" is "soul." This verse says that every
beast has a soul.

God *made* every beast wherein there is soul, as well as
man. The question we must now ask is where is the soul-
life of man. Leviticus tells us.

Leviticus 17:11:
For the life of the flesh *is* in the blood . . . .

The soul-life is in the blood and is passed on to the
next generation when the sperm impregnates the egg at
the time of fertilization. Then, at birth when the child
takes his first breath, he becomes an independent living
soul. And when a person takes his last breath his soul is
gone, his life is over.

As God progressed in this work of forming, making
and creating the earth and its inhabitants, He finally
came to bringing about his culminating work — man.
Now after studying "formed" and "made," we still must
consider the biblical usage of the word "created." What
part of man was created?

Genesis 1:27:
So God created man in his *own* image, in the image of God
created he him; male and female created he them.

God formed the body of man and made his soul. What was God doing when He created man in His own image? What is the image of God?

John 4:24:
God *is* a Spirit . . . .

Thus, God's image is spirit. God created, *bara*, spirit within man. With this act man became body, soul and spirit. After God created within man His own image, God had a companion — not in the body and soul parts of man, but in the spirit. However, in God's giving man a spirit, man did not become God the Creator or co-equal with the Lord God.[1] Yet because of God's spirit in man, men are occasionally in the Old Testament called gods.[2] God is Spirit, and when He gave His spirit to man, it became possible for God to talk to man and for man to communicate with God. This gave them fellowship.

In God's communication with Adam, God oriented the first human to the rules of life. The only restriction which God put on Adam is recorded in Genesis 2.

Genesis 2:16 and 17:
And the Lord God commanded the man, saying, Of every tree of the garden thou mayest freely eat:

But of the tree of the knowledge of good and evil, thou shalt

---

1. God had more direct involvement in bringing about the first Adam than the second Adam, Jesus Christ.
2. See Chapter Two, pages 32 and 33.

not eat of it: for in the day [not *a* day, but in *that very day*] that thou eatest thereof thou shalt surely die.

How does Weirwille know this?

In the beginning there was only one who was above Adam, and that was God. Except for God, Adam was the chief being. As earth's ruler, Adam had only one God-forbidden act with the consequences being "... for in the day that thou eatest thereof thou shalt surely die."

The natural man[3] of body and soul has only his five senses whereby he can acquire natural knowledge. In contrast, the first man not only could gain knowledge through his five senses, but he could also ascertain knowledge through his communication with God, made possible by God's creation of spirit within him. Adam thus had two means by which he could learn and know, and he had the freedom of will to choose whether he was going to gather knowledge by his five senses or by the spirit — God's revelation to him.

When God created spirit within man, man could have perfect fellowship with the Creator at all times. God furthermore elevated His companion by giving him supreme power on earth over certain things which God designated.

---

3. When the Bible speaks of the man of body and soul, it refers to the man who is *not* born again of God's Spirit. This is the "natural man," biblically speaking. For the natural man, the five senses are the sole avenues of learning. Everything that comes to his mind comes by one or a combination of the five senses.

Genesis 1:26:
... Let them [mankind] have dominion over the fish of the sea, and over the fowl of the air, and over the cattle, and over all the earth.

Where Wieu get mind?

Adam had dominion over the earth; and as long as Adam walked by the spirit, he had perfect fellowship with God. But the moment Adam chose to let his senses rule his mind and body instead of walking by the spirit, calamity resulted. Why? Because then he was no longer God-ruled. Adam had had the option of walking by his senses or walking by the spirit, and he determined by his free will to be led by what he could see, hear, smell, taste and touch rather than to be led by God.

all of this is inferred

Genesis tells the story of how Adam and his helpmate Eve chose to walk by their senses. Remember that Lucifer, who had fallen, is also called the serpent.

Genesis 3:1:
Now the serpent was more subtil than any beast of the field which the Lord God had made. And he said unto the woman, Yea, hath God said, Ye shall not eat of every tree of the garden?

Did the serpent know what God had said? He knew perfectly well. With this knowledge, the serpent went to Eve and said, "Did God really say, 'You shall not eat of every tree of the garden?'"

Genesis 3:6:

And when the woman saw that the tree *was* good for food, and that it *was* pleasant to the eyes [the senses], and a tree to be desired to make *one* wise, she took of the fruit thereof, and did eat, and gave also unto her husband with her; and he did eat.

Thus man fell because of disobedience to God's Word. God's Word said, "You can do this, but not this." The Devil said, "You just go ahead and do it because you will be just as wise as God." The Bible says that Eve was deceived by the Devil.[4] Adam was never deceived;[5] he simply followed Eve's example.

Adam's mistake was cataclysmic for God had clearly stated, "For in the day that thou eatest thereof thou shalt surely die." What died on the day Adam and Eve ate of the tree of knowledge of good and evil? Did Adam and Eve still have bodies and souls? Certainly. What they no longer had was their connection with God, spirit. This is why God said, "The day that thou eatest thereof thou shalt surely die."

Many times we have heard it said, "Well, they didn't really die. It was just the seed of death that was planted in them because the Word of God tells that Adam lived approximately 800 years after the paradise expulsion."

4. Genesis 3:13: "And the Lord God said unto the woman, What *is* this *that* thou hast done? And the woman said, The serpent beguiled me, and I did eat."
5. I Timothy 2:14: "And Adam was not deceived, but the woman being deceived was in the transgression."

The Word does not agree with this seeds-of-death ex-
planation. The Word says, "the day [the very day] that
thou eatest thereof thou shalt surely [absolutely] die."
One must understand the man of body, soul and spirit
to be aware of exactly what happened on the day that
Adam defied God's one rule.

The spirit departed from Adam. The reason the spirit
was called dead is that it was no longer there. Adam and
Eve's spiritual connection with God was lost. From that
very day they returned to just body and soul people,
natural men.

Man, being body and soul, then had no choice but to
rely entirely on his five senses for learning. From the
day Adam ate of the tree of knowledge of good and evil
until the day of Pentecost thousands of years later,
whenever God wanted to communicate with man He
had to come into concretion. He had to come into some
form for the man's senses to perceive and thereby
understand. For example, Moses, traveling along in the
wilderness, saw a burning bush; and from the midst of
the burning bush, he heard a voice. Moses' senses perceived God. The children of Israel could see the Ten
Commandments. This was the means by which God
came into concrete form to tell them what to do. An-
nually, on the Day of Atonement, the high priest entered
into the Holy of Holies to make sacrifices. He laid his
hands on the goat outside the temple and then sent it
into the wilderness to die. God had said that as surely as

the Israelites saw the goat go into the wilderness so certainly their sins went with it. They could see the goat, they could see the stone tablet, they could see the burning bush.

God had to use concrete forms because men had no means by which to understand spiritual things. But since man still had the five senses, he could believe when his senses experienced stimuli. This explains why Jesus Christ was born. So that people in the senses world could know God, Jesus Christ had to be manifested in physical form.[6] Jesus said, "... He that hath seen me hath seen the Father," meaning that Jesus Christ was the Father's will in manifestation. God was *in* Christ reconciling the world unto Himself. Jesus Christ was the concretion.

When God made man and gave him freedom of choice to follow God's will, the true God and His arch-enemy the Devil became involved in all-out combat. If Adam and Eve had been allowed to stay in Paradise after the fall, the Devil would have eternally defeated God.

Genesis 3:22 and 23:
And the Lord God said, Behold, the man is become as one of

---

6. The burning bush and the stone tablets were just as much the manifestation of God as was Jesus Christ. God sent them just as He sent Jesus Christ. Yet it is obvious that they were not with God in the beginning in the heavenlies. So why do some believe that Jesus Christ had to literally be with God from the beginning? Jesus Christ was simply God's revealing Himself by His Son who before He was born only existed in God's foreknowledge, just as the bush did or the stone tablets did.

us, to know good and evil: and now, lest he put forth his hand, and take also of the tree of life, and eat, and live for ever:

Therefore the Lord God sent him forth from the garden of Eden, to till the ground from whence he was taken.

The Devil could then have kept man in an unredeemable state of sin forever if man had eaten of the tree of life after once sinning. So that this would not happen, God drove Adam and Eve out of the garden or paradise.

As a result of Adam's fall, God invoked a plan to legally redeem man from his fallen state. God, who is just, would never simply "kidnap" man back from the Devil and the fallen state; but rather, being a just God, He had to redeem man on legal grounds. Genesis 3:15 gives the first prophecy of such a plan.

And I will put enmity between thee [speaking to the serpent] and the woman, and between thy seed and her seed; it shall bruise thy head, and thou shalt bruise his heel.

To fulfill this prophecy, God made preparation before the foundation of the world to have a Son. The record of the conception and birth of Jesus Christ is clearly set forth in Matthew 1:18-25.

Now the birth of Jesus Christ was on this wise: When as his mother Mary was espoused to Joseph, before they came to together, she was found with child of the Holy Ghost.

Then Joseph her husband, being a just *man,* and not willing to make her a publick example, was minded to put her away privily.

But while he thought on these things, behold, the angel of the Lord appeared unto him in a dream, saying, Joseph, thou son of David, fear not to take unto thee Mary thy wife: for that which is conceived in her is of the Holy Ghost.

And she shall bring forth a son, and thou shalt call his name JESUS: for he shall save his people from their sins.

Now all this was done, that it might be fulfilled which was spoken of the Lord by the prophet, saying,

Behold, a virgin shall be with child, and shall bring forth a son, and they shall call his name Emmanuel, which being interpreted is, God with us.

Then Joseph being raised from sleep did as the angel of the Lord had bidden him, and took unto him his wife:

And knew her not till she had brought forth her firstborn son: and he called his name JESUS.

There is no question that the Bible teaches divine conception. The question pertains only to the integrity of the Bible. The Bible also teaches that all men since Adam are born "dead in trespasses and sin," while at the same time claiming that Jesus was a sinless man. Jesus was born sinless, but he also maintained himself sinless as he grew older. How can we account for the original sinlessness of Jesus — that he was born sinless? Hebrews gives part of the answer.

Hebrews 2:14:
Forasmuch then as the children are partakers of flesh and blood, he [Jesus] also himself likewise took part of the same ....

All children are of Adam, and all partake of Adam's flesh and blood.[7] The word "partake" is the Greek word *koinōneō* and means "to share fully." So all of Adam's decendants *share fully* in his flesh and blood, thereby transmitting sinfulness to all Adam's children. But Jesus just "took part" of the same; the Greek word is *metechō* which means "to take only a part, not all." Jesus took some part, but not all; he did not share fully, *koinōneō*. According to the flesh, he was of Mary; but the life of the flesh in the blood of Jesus came by way of supernatural conception by the Holy Spirit, God.

If Jesus had been conceived from an ovum of Mary and a sperm of Joseph, he would have been as sinful as any other child and would have shared fully in Adam's flesh and blood. But the genes with the dominant characteristics came to Jesus not through Mary but by way of the creation of a sperm by God and thus he could have sinless blood.

---

7. Flesh when used as a figure of speech stands for physical body, while blood represents life.

Natural life, called soul-life, is in the blood.[8] Sin is transmitted through the soul-life and not through the physical flesh which is simply the vehicle that manifests sin. This life which is in the blood is contributed by the sperm of the male. Soul-life is carried in the seed. You can understand the important significance of the male's contribution when studying the conception of Jesus Christ.

The ovum has to be fertilized by the sperm to have soul-life. The mother provides the unborn, developing infant with the nutritive elements for the building of that little body within her. All the nutritive elements and even antibodies pass freely from mother to fetus through the placenta, along with the waste products of the child's metabolism which pass back to the mother. Normally, however, there is no actual interchange of blood. All the blood which is in that child is produced within the fetus itself.

How wonderfully God prepared for the birth of His Son, Jesus Christ, from the beginning. When He formed and made woman, He made her so that no blood should pass directly from her to her offspring.

Adam is the head of all the races of men on earth, and Jesus had to be of the line of Adam in order to fulfill the law. God, to produce a sinless man and yet one who was of the line of Adam, had to provide a way whereby Jesus would have a human body derived from

_____

8. Leviticus 17:11: "For the life of the flesh *is* in the blood ...."

Adam and yet not have soul-life from Adam's sinful blood.[9]

Mary nurtured the embryo of Jesus in her womb, and thus he was of the line of Adam and David according to the flesh. But the Holy Spirit contributed the soul-life in the blood of Jesus by way of the sperm. In Jesus' arteries and veins there was sinless soul-life. When Judas betrayed Jesus he confessed, according to Matthew 27:4, "I have betrayed the innocent blood." Sin made man's soul-life corruptible, but the soul-life of Jesus was from God.

> Luke 1:35:
> And the angel answered and said unto her, The Holy Ghost shall come upon thee, and the power of the Highest shall overshadow thee: therefore also that holy thing which shall be born of thee shall be called the Son of God.

God cannot be born but His Son, our Lord and Savior Jesus Christ, was conceived in Mary by God's creation. Thus the conception of Jesus Christ was a miracle by supernatural laws, but the birth proceeded according to natural laws.

If Jesus Christ had had the same source of soul-life as all other men, he could not have legally redeemed man for he would not have been a perfect sacrifice. Similarly

---

9. God created the sperm that impregnated the ovum (egg) of Mary in the Fallopian tube. This created sperm carried only dominant characteristics and did what ordinarily any sperm would do to an impregnated ovum. See V.P. Wierwille, "The Genealogy of Jesus Christ," *The Word's Way* (New Knoxville, Ohio: American Christian Press, 1971).

if Jesus Christ had been God, he would not have legally redeemed man for he could not have wilfully chosen to do so.

If God did not care to act within legal boundaries, He could have rectified the situation immediately after Adam and Eve's fall. But, had God done this, he would not have been all good and all perfect.

Romans 5:12-14:[10]

Mark what follows. It was through one man that sin entered the world, and through sin death, and thus death pervaded the whole human race, inasmuch as all men have sinned.

For sin was already in the world before there was law, though in the absence of law no reckoning is kept of sin.

But death held sway from Adam to Moses, even over those who had not sinned as Adam did, by disobeying a direct command -- and Adam foreshadows the Man who was to come.

Note the consequences to mankind as a result of Adam's fall as recorded in Genesis. The word "foreshadow" in the above is the word "figure" in the King James. Verse 14 says that Adam was the figure of him that was to come. The Greek word for "figure" is *tupos* from which is derived the English word "type." Adam was the first man and the type; Christ, who came, was the second man.

---

10. The following quotations from Romans 5 are all taken from the New English Translation.

Verses 15-17:

But God's act of grace is out of all proportion to Adam's wrongdoing. For if the wrongdoing of that one man brought death upon so many, its effect is vastly exceeded by the grace of God and the gift that came to so many by the grace of the one man, Jesus Christ.

And again, the gift of God is not to be compared in its effect with that one man's sin; for the judicial action, following upon the one offence, issued in a verdict of condemnation, but the act of grace, following upon so many misdeeds, issued in a verdict of acquittal.

For if by the wrongdoing of that one man death established its reign, through a single sinner, much more shall those who receive in far greater measure God's grace, and his gift of righteousness, live and reign through the one man, Jesus Christ.

Notice the distinction in the results of the works of these two men —— the first man, Adam, and the second man, Jesus Christ. The result of the one man's work was death; the result of the other was life. Then verses 18 through 21 of this fifth chapter of Romans sum up the entire situation.

It follows, then, that as the issue of one misdeed was condemnation for all men, so the issue of one just act is acquittal and life for all men.

For as through the disobedience of the one man the many were made sinners, so through the obedience of the one man the many will be made righteous.

Law intruded into this process to multiply law-breaking. But where sin was thus multiplied, grace immeasurably exceeded it, in order that, as sin established its reign by way of death, so God's grace might establish its reign in righteousness, and issue in eternal life through Jesus Christ our Lord.

When we stop and take a careful look at the accuracy of God's wonderful Word, we can't avoid seeing what God has done for us through Christ's sacrifice. Jesus Christ brought righteousness because he willingly gave himself as a perfect, sinless sacrifice, a perfect redeemer.

I Corinthians 5:7:
. . . For even Christ our passover is sacrificed for us.

To understand our redemption through Christ our passover, we must know that the perfect sacrifice had to be a man and not God.

God accomplished seven things by His Son, Jesus Christ, to bring about our redemption: (1) the birth of Jesus Christ; (2) his sinless life; (3) the death of Jesus Christ on the cross;[11] (4) his resurrection three days and three nights later; (5) his ministry following the resurrection; (6) Christ's ascension; and, finally, (7) the coming of holy spirit on the day of Pentecost. Had any one of these parts not taken place, our lives would not be totally redeemed.

---

11. The Word of God says that Jesus Christ was dead for 72 hours. How could Jesus Christ be God for God cannot die? He is Alpha and Omega.

One of the seven accomplishments of Jesus Christ is his death, thereby becoming our passover. Compare the death of Jesus Christ to the passover lamb of Israel. At the precedent-setting, first passover, God commanded Moses to instruct the children of Israel about the sacrificial lamb.

Exodus 12:5:
Your lamb shall be without blemish, a male of the first year: ye shall take *it* out from the sheep, or from the goats.

It was so important that the lamb be "without blemish." Therefore, for Christ to be our passover he would have to meet all of the qualifications of the blemishless passover lamb.

The Word of God refers to Jesus as the Lamb of God.

John 1:29:
Behold the Lamb of God, which taketh away the sin of the world.

Jesus Christ was this perfect lamb that "taketh away the sin of the world," as told in I Peter 1.

I Peter 1:18 and 19:
Forasmuch as ye know that ye were not redeemed with corruptible things, *as* silver and gold, from your vain conversation *received* by tradition from your fathers;

But with the precious blood of Christ, as of a lamb without blemish and without spot.

Jesus Christ was without blemish and without spot. Furthermore, the male passover lamb was to be taken out from among the sheep. This is why Jesus Christ had to be a man. He had to be one of the flock. God could not have died for our sins; God could never have been nailed to a cross. God is Spirit; God is not a sheep from the flock. Jesus Christ, His only-begotten Son, was the lamb from the flock.

When people begin to comprehend the accuracy of God's Word concerning "Christ our passover," their minds cannot help but stand in amazement and their hearts thrill at the greatness of God and His only-begotten Son, our Redeemer, Jesus Christ.

It took the shed blood of a lamb to save the Israelites from destruction. If the blood of one little lamb could save an entire house from damnation, think of what the shedding of Christ's blood did for you and me.

Hebrews 9:13-15:
For if the blood of bulls and of goats, and the ashes of an heifer sprinkling the unclean, sanctifieth to the purifying of the flesh:

How much more shall the blood of Christ, who through the eternal Spirit offered himself without spot to God, purge your conscience from dead works to serve the living God?

And for this cause, he is the mediator of the new testament, that by means of death, for the redemption of the transgressions *that were* under the first testament, they which are called might receive the promise of eternal inheritance.

Christ met every fulfillment of the law.[12] The greatness of God's Word shows how through his death and sacrifices Jesus Christ was our passover. To accomplish this, Jesus Christ had to be a man. He had to be a lamb from the flock.[13] He had to be sacrificed under that law so that we might live in the liberty of the spirit of life in Christ Jesus.

Those who teach that Jesus Christ is God and God is Jesus Christ will never stand approved in "rightly dividing" God's Word, for there is only one God, and "thou shalt have no other gods." The Bible clearly teaches that Jesus Christ was a man conceived by the Holy Spirit, God, whose life was without blemish and without spot, a lamb from the flock, thereby being the perfect sacrifice. Thus he became our redeemer.

12. Romans 10:4: "Christ *is* the end of the law for righteousness to every one that believeth."
13. Hebrews 9:14 states that Christ the blemishless lamb offered himself to God. God would not offer Himself to Himself. But Christ was not God; and, therefore, presented himself to God as the perfect sacrifice.

CHAPTER FOUR

WHO IS THE WORD?

S ince the early centuries after Christ, Christian doctrine in many instances has taught that Jesus was co-
existent and co-equal with God; Jesus either in Spirit or
in some other form was with God from the beginning.
The people who hold or have held this idea that
God is Jesus and Jesus is God substantiate their beliefs
by isolating bits of biblical texts. Genesis 1:26 is their
initial scripture where God says, "Let us make man in
our image ...." "Us" and "our" are interpreted to mean
"God in conjunction with Jesus Christ."

Truly, this scripture is no proof of Jesus' existence in
the beginning. The first person plural pronouns, "we"
and "us," are used to indicate the magnitude of the
incident to which God related Himself. When a plural
noun or pronoun is used but the singular case is true

to fact, it is the figure of speech *heterosis.* The plural is used for the singular when great excellence or magnitude is denoted.[1] Monarchs use the plural pronoun when speaking of themselves in their official positions. For example, to this very day, the English ruler uses the expression "we" when speaking of herself in her official capacity. In this same grammatical sense, God employed the plural pronouns and personal adjectives: "Let US make man in OUR image, after OUR likeness ...."

The Bible teaches that there is only one true God, that God was *in* Christ,[2] that God is Spirit,[3] and that God is eternal in contrast to Jesus whose beginning was his birth.

Aside from the "we" of Genesis 1:26, the basic scripture upon which the Jesus-is-God doctrine has been founded is John 1:1. This has been read and interpreted as follows: "In the beginning was God the Father, God the Son, God the Holy Ghost. All three were with God, and all three were God." But this is not what the verse says.

---

1. E.W. Bullinger, *Figures of Speech Used in the Bible.* (London: Messrs Eyre and Spottiswoode, 1898), p. 529.
2. II Corinthians 5:19: "To wit, that God was in Christ, reconciling the world unto himself, not imputing their trespasses unto them; and hath committed unto us the word of reconciliation."
3. John 4:24: "God *is* a Spirit: and they that worship him must worship *him* in spirit and in truth."

In the beginning was the Word, and the Word was with God, and the Word was God.

The question of John 1:1 is who is "the Word" or what is "the Word" (*logos*). Genesis 1:1 plainly states, "In the beginning God ...." God alone was from the beginning.

How does God who is Spirit communicate Himself as "the Word," *logos,* with man who is flesh? Human beings communicate with each other by way of symbols, be they spoken words, pictures or sign language. These symbols communicate ideas and thoughts. But Spirit cannot communicate with mind, senses or reason as spirit and senses are two separate and well-defined categories.

John 3:6—8:
That which is born of the flesh is flesh; and that which is born of the Spirit is spirit.

Marvel not that I said unto thee, Ye must be born again.

The wind bloweth where it listeth, and thou hearest the sound thereof, but canst not tell whence it cometh, and whither it goeth: so is every one that is born of the Spirit.

Spirit and flesh are in two different realms and each one must stay within its own boundaries. Spirit can communicate with spirit only, and flesh by way of the senses can communicate only with the senses or the material realm. How then does God overcome these communication barriers?

God who is Spirit manifests Himself to men in three ways: (1) by His spirit, which was upon special people in the Old Testament and which is in those who are born again during this the age of grace; (2) by His only-begotten Son, Jesus Christ; (3) by His Word, both the written and spoken.

God, to manifest Himself in the world of the flesh, had to use a concrete form for senses men to recognize. God gave the revealed Word so that man by his natural faculties might be able to understand the communication from God. When John 1:1 says, "... and the Word was with God," it refers to the manifested, revealed *logos*: (1) the written Word which has come to us as the Bible and (2) the created Word which is Jesus Christ. "In the beginning was the Word [God] and the [revealed] Word was with God ...."

How was this revealed Word with God? The Word was with God in His foreknowledge.[4] God is omniscient, knowing all things: He knew from before the foundation of the world that the man which He formed, made and created would sin; He knew from before the foundation of the world that Jesus Christ would redeem man; He knew from before the foundation of the world that it would be possible for man to be born again; He knows our end as well as our beginning. This is what

4. See Chapter Two, pages 28-30.

John 1:1 literally says: The revealed "Word was with God" in His foreknowledge; the revealed Word was later to be manifested in writing as the Bible and in the flesh as Jesus Christ.

How was Jesus with God in the beginning? In the same way that the written Word was with Him, namely, in God's foreknowledge. The reason Jesus Christ is the Word and is called in the Bible the *logos* is that he was God's plan for man's redemption and salvation. The subject of the entire Bible is God who revealed Himself most completely in His Son, Jesus Christ, the redeemer of man. In the Old Testament, Jesus Christ was in God's foreknowledge and in the foreknowledge of God's people as God revealed this prophetic knowledge to them. When Jesus Christ was born, he came into existence. Foreknowledge became a reality.

God, who is Spirit, in order to manifest Himself in concretion, had to reveal Himself and His will in words and in His Son. God's communication of Himself as the *logos*, the revealed written and spoken Word, came into manifestation when "... holy men of God spake *as they were* moved by the Holy Ghost."[5] And, when the fullness of time came, Jesus Christ who was God's communication of Himself in the flesh was born.[6]

---

5. II Peter 1:21: "For the prophecy came not in old time by the will of man: but holy men of God spake *as they were* moved by the Holy Ghost."
6. John 1:14: "And the Word was made flesh, and dwelt among us, (and we beheld his glory, the glory as of the only begotten of the Father,) full of grace and truth."

John 1:2:

The same was in the beginning with God.

"The same" is this revealed Word which was with God in His foreknowledge from the very beginning. Verse 2 is a repetition of what we just noted in verse 1. Why the repetition? To establish what has been said. Whenever God doubles a revelation in the Word, the absoluteness is established.[7] This truth concerning the revealed Word is so great, so magnificent and so wonderful that God had it stated twice to emphasize it and to indicate the definite establishment of it.

The preposition "with" in verses 1 and 2 of John 1 further confirms this whole truth: "... And the Word was with [*pros*] God .... The same was in the beginning with [*pros*] God." There are a vast number of different Greek prepositions translated "with," but only *pros* could fit here. *Pros* means "together with and yet having distinct independence"; "intimate and close inter-communion, together with distinct independence." The revealed Word was together *with* God and yet distinctly independent of Him. This removes the guessing from John 1:1 and 2 and fits it together with the laws used in language as well as harmonizing the truth with the rest of the Word of God.

---

7. Genesis 41:32: "And for that the dream was doubled unto Pharaoh twice: *it is* because the thing *is* established by God."

John 1:1 and 2:
In the beginning was the Word [God], and the [revealed]
Word was with [*pros*] God [with Him in His foreknowledge,
yet independent of Him], and the Word was God.

The same [revealed Word] was in the beginning with [*pros*]
God.

Verse 2 could literally read, "The same [the written
Word, which is the Bible, and the Word in the flesh,
which is Jesus Christ] was in the beginning with God [in
His foreknowledge].

The following scriptures enable us to more fully
understand God's communication to man by way of the
prophets who gave us the written Word and by His Son
Jesus Christ who was sent by God.

Psalms 107:20:
He [God] sent his word [by way of the phophets], and healed
them ....

John 5:36:
... the same works that I do, bear witness of me, that the
Father hath sent me.

John 5:38:
And ye have not his word abiding in you: for whom he hath
sent, him ye believe not.

John 17:3:

... that they might know thee the only true God, and Jesus
Christ, whom thou hast sent.

The first phrase in John 1:1, "In the beginning" is a
significant usage of words. The word "beginning" can be
used in two ways. First of all a person could speak of
the beginning of a football game in terms of the
moment the game begins. In such a case one would say
that the players were on the field from the beginning of
the game. However, in a more active sense, someone
could speak of the beginning of the game as all the
preliminary events which lead up to the game including
the training of the players, the preparation of the sta-
dium, the practicing of the cheerleaders and all other
events involved in getting ready for that game. This
second usage is the one employed in this first verse of
John. "In the beginning ...."

Notice that the first word in the verse is "in," not
"from." The Greek word is *en*. If *ek* or *apo* had been
used meaning "out from" or "away from," a specific
point, the time of a definite beginning would have been
indicated. The "in," *en*, of John 1:1 is "in" or "during
the beginning," *en archē*, before the heavens and earth
were created. God, who was in the beginning and who
was the *logos*, is eternal. Jesus Christ, who is God's
communication of Himself in a person, had a beginning
when he was born, yet in God's foreknowledge Jesus

Christ was in the beginning.

The word for "word" in John 1:1 is *logos* preceded by the article *ho*. Another Greek word *rhēma*, which is also translated "word," indicates a reference only to the words which are spoken, implying nothing as to the thought or meaning conveyed by the words. However, the word *logos* does not just mean the sound itself but the thought and idea that is conveyed by the word or words. In John 1:1 the *logos*, which is God, has reference to the thoughts and ideas conveyed by the spoken Words, the written Words and the incarnate Word. All the spoken, written and incarnate Words were with God in His foreknowledge. They did not come into existence in the senses world until God had someone with whom to communicate. In the beginning (before the creation of the world), the Word, *logos*, was God and this Word, *logos*, was with God in His foreknowledge. It was first communicated to man by the spoken and written Word and later by the incarnate Word, His Son Jesus Christ.

In the next phrase of this first verse of John, we again find the same usage of the word *logos.* However this time *logos* is coupled with the prepositional phrase "with God." This "with" is the unique usage of the word *pros,* and the word "God" is employed with a definite article. In other words, the Word was together with yet distinctly independent of *the* God. There is only one true God who is above all and who was in the beginning. The definite article is employed in the Greek to bring out this distinction that He is *the* one true God. The Word, which was with God in the beginning in His foreknowledge and which was later spoken, written and made incarnate, had been together with the one true God in His foreknowledge yet distinctly independent of Him.

The third phrase "the Word was God" ties together the first two phrases in this verse. The word "God" has no article for grammatical reasons rather than thought content. "The Word, which was with God in His foreknowledge and later became spoken, written and incarnate, was God." God is His Word the same as you are your word and I am my word. My words are my communication of my thoughts, feelings and ideas to you. Similarly, God's Word is His thoughts and ideas communicated to us. When I make a statement and my word is my will, then my words are just as much a part of me as is my body.

Verse 2:
The same was in the beginning with God.

In verse 2 the first two words "the same" are the one Greek word *houtos.* This word is a demonstrative pronoun normally translated by the English word "this" and refers back to the nearest associated noun, pointing out and bringing special emphasis to that noun. The antecedent in this case is *logos,* the Word which was God.

The words "in the beginning," *en archē,* are the same as in verse 1, indicating the situation before the creation in Genesis 1. Again the phrase "with the God," *pros tou theou,* shows that the Word was together with God in His foreknowledge yet distinctly independent of the one true God. All three clauses in verse 1 are cemented together in this one clause of verse 2, thereby doubling God's declaration regarding Himself and His Word. The certainty of the reality is thereby established beyond a shadow of a doubt.

A literal translation according to the usage of the words in verses 1 and 2 of this great first chapter of John reads as follows: "In the beginning (before the creation) God was the Word, and the revealed Word was in God's foreknowledge (which was later communicated to man in spoken Words, written Words and the incarnate Word). This Word absolutely was in the beginning before the foundation of the world together with the one true God in His foreknowledge yet distinctly independent of Him."

Verse 3 continues the information divulged in the first two verses of John 1.

All things were made by him [God] ; and without him [God] was not any thing made that was made.

"Him" is the pronoun *autou* controlled by its closest associated noun which is "God." Therefore, we must always remember that only God was in the beginning as stated in Genesis 1:1.

The usage of the word "all" is always used in one of two ways. It either indicates "all without exception" or "all with distinction." "All without exception" means there are absolutely no exceptions to what is stated. But "all with distinction" means that there are no exceptions within a certain group; however, there are exceptions outside of that particular group. The "all" employed in this verse is "all without exception," since all things without exception were made by God.

The words "not anything" are the Greek *oude hen* which literally means "not even one." So the latter part of this verse corroborates the fact that there is not even one exception.

The words "was made" are the Greek word *egeneto* which means "to bring about" or "to come into being." The verb form is in the aorist tense indicating the singleness of the action which happened in Genesis chapter one. God brought everything into existence. He was the cause or the sole mover of everything that was created.

The phrase "by him" further corroborates this. The word "by" is the Greek preposition *dia* which, when indicating instrument or means, is translated "by," the cause of the action. God was the cause of the creation.

The manner in which all things were made by the Word of God, who was the cause of the action, is clearly illustrated in Genesis 1 where God says, "Let there be .... And there was ...." What God said always came about. It was His Word that caused all things to come into reality.

While the first two verbs translated "made" in verse 3 are in the aorist tense indicating the singleness of God's action, the third and last verb "made" is in the perfect tense and refers to anything that both was made in the past and which exists in the present, bringing an emphasis to everything that has been created, formed and made. Nothing has come into existence without God's being the Creator.

Verse 3 clearly marks the beginning of the world that we know, whereas verses 1 and 2 mark that time which was in the beginning before the foundation of the world. In the beginning, only God and the Word in His foreknowledge were in existence.

A literal translation according to usage of words in verse 3 is: "All things without exception were made by God who was the cause of their existence. And without God not one thing came into being that has existed or does exist presently."

John 1:4:
In him [God] was life; and the life was the light of men.

What was this life which was in God and which was the light of men? This life was the spirit from God, the light of God given in concretion. The spirit from God was upon all the prophets who spoke and wrote God's mind and will; finally, it was upon Jesus Christ himself.[8] The spirit from God made possible spiritual revelation from God to men of God. Not everything that God revealed to the prophets was written. Prophets frequently spoke the Word of God and did not commit it to writing. At other times the prophets wrote what they had earlier spoken. Some of the spoken words of the prophets we do not have, but the Word we do have in writing was and still is "the light of men."

Not everything that God has revealed to man is recorded in the Bible, but that which is needed for salvation and for our learning is recorded.[9] This is the meaning of the statement in John 1:4: "... and the life was the light of men."

John 1:5:
And the light [God[10]] shineth in darkness; and the darkness comprehended it not.

How did the light shine in darkness before the coming of Jesus Christ? By way of the men of God who spoke or wrote God's mind and will. The written Word continues today to shine in the darkness of this world. Darkness cannot bring forth light, neither can darkness

8. Mark 1:10: "And straightway coming up out of the water, he saw the heavens open, and the Spirit like a dove descending upon him."

9. II Peter 1:3: "According as his divine power hath given unto us all things that *pertain* unto life and godliness, through the knowledge of him that hath called us to glory and virtue:

10. I John 1:5: "This then is the message which we have heard of him, and declare unto you, that God is light, and in him is no darkness at all."

overcome light. Even one small candle is powerful enough to penetrate and dispel darkness. So also is God's revelation of Himself in His Word: "the darkness comprehended it not"; the darkness could not extinguish the light.

The clause in verse 5 is a general rather than a specific statement regarding light and darkness. It does not refer to a specific time in the past, in the present or in the future, but rather it is making a generalization about all time. Darkness is the absence of light. Light, heat and all forms of energy are measured in terms of the positive, never the negative. The negative is the absence of the positive. Even from a scientific point of view there is no way that darkness could comprehend light since darkness is the absence of light. That which does not exist cannot overcome that which exists.

seems rather obvious

John 1:6-8:
There was a man sent [*apostellō*] from God, whose name *was* John.

The same [John] came for a witness, to bear witness of the Light [God], that all *men* through him [John] might believe.

He [John] was not that Light [God], but *was sent* to bear witness of that Light [God].

The ministry of John the Baptist is given in these three verses. God commissioned John for the special purpose of bearing witness. He came specifically to carry forth the sender's message and was the forerunner of Jesus Christ by the timing of his birth.

> John 1:9:
> *That* was the true Light [God], which lighteth every man that cometh into the world.

God is the "true light." How does God "light" every man who comes into the world? By His revealed Word. God's revealed Word continues to light every man, even the unbeliever. Without the "true light" this would be a totally impenetrable world of darkness.

The true light is the life that is in the *logos* which was manifested to man by the written Word, the spoken Word and the incarnate Word, Jesus Christ, as these three means gradually revealed God throughout time. However, before the Word was revealed, it existed only in God's foreknowledge.

The focal point of the opening verses in the Gospel of John sets before us with utmost clarity the centrality of God. We note the added emphasis on God in the following verse.

> John 1:10:
> He [God] was in the world [by the revealed Word], and the world was made by him [God], and the world knew him [God] not.

Let us take the time to trace the pronouns and nouns in verses 10 back to their origin. The words "he" and "him" in this verse are the pronouns under consideration. From the Greek they could be either neuter or masculine; in this case they must be neuter since the nearest associated noun would be the true light of verse 9. The true light which was the light of men in verse 4 was the life that was in him. The "him" of verse 4 refers back to the Word which was God in verses 1, 2 and 3. Therefore, it is God who is His Word which has the life in Him, the true light which was in the world through the spoken or written Word and later the incarnate Word, Jesus Christ. In the Old Testament it was the spoken Word and written Word which came into the world; yet the world did not receive or believe God's Word, therefore, it could not know God.

John 1:11:
He [God] came unto his own [Israel], and his own received him not.

God through His Word came unto His own people, which was Israel. He did this by both His spoken and His written Word. Later He came to His own through His Son Jesus Christ who was the incarnate Word. However, God's own people did not receive that Word. The words "his own" are the Greek words *ta idia* in the first usage and *hoi idioi* in the second usage in this verse. The former, in Greek, is the neuter gender while the latter is the masculine gender. God came unto "his own things," that is to His own possessions or those things which were His. But His own people did not receive His Word, in either its spoken or written or incarnate form.

> John 1:12:
> But as many [of Israel] as received him [God], to them gave he [God] power [*exousia*, authority, the right] to become the sons of God, *even* to them that believe on [unto] his name [namesake, Jesus Christ].

Again tracing our nouns and pronouns back, we find that as many as received Him -- who was the true light which was the life in the Word -- God gave them power to become the children of God by adoption. If they received God's Word, they received God. If they did not receive God's Word, they did not receive God. The means by which God gave them power to become children by adoption was to believe on His namesake, the Word which would become incarnate, which was Jesus Christ. "Jesus" in the Hebrew means "God our Saviour." Jesus Christ was God's Son and was named for His Father. It is unto that namesake, Jesus Christ, that Israel had to believe to be saved, as prophesied in the Old Testament.

The word "on" -- "to them that believe on" – is the preposition *eis*, meaning "unto." Euclid, the mathematician, used the word *eis* as showing motion along a line from a starting point to the point at which one wished to arrive. This usage in verse 12 then says, " ... to them who continue believing unto [continuously continue to believe on] his name ...." Israel remained as adopted sons so long as they continued believing. The Israelites were not sons of God by birth; but when Israel believed "unto [*eis*] His name," God adopted them as sons.

"Even to them that believe on his name" refers to the name of Jesus Christ, which is above every other human name. He, Jesus Christ, was the "namesake" of God, which name relates back to the source of all life, God.

A literal translation according to usage of verse 12 would be: "But as many as walked according to the revealed Word given to the prophets and later the revealed Word, Jesus Christ, to them God gave the privilege of adoption as sons of God, to those who continued believing unto the name of Jesus Christ."

John 1:13:
Which were [who was] born [conceived], not of blood, nor of the will of the flesh, nor of the will of man, but of God.

The first word, "which," must be the word "who," referring to the "namesake" of verse 12, Jesus Christ. There are no manuscripts indicating this although second century writers ascribed to it which shows that an earlier text must have had a rendering of "who" instead of "which." An itacism of this nature or text corruption due to misunderstanding is not uncommon. Nevertheless, this scripture must be in harmony with all related scriptures.

The word "born" is the same word as "begotten": "Who was born [begotten], not of blood ...." You and I are born of blood. All Israel was born of blood. Hebrews 2:14 says, "... children are partakers of flesh and blood ...." The only one who did not partake as the natural man in the life of the flesh, which is in the blood, was Jesus Christ. Therefore, John 1:13 refers only to Jesus Christ. It was Jesus Christ "who was born, not of blood, nor of the will of the flesh, nor of the will of man, but of God." Jesus Christ was conceived by God's creating soul-life. God created, brought into existence, a sperm in an ovum in Mary.

There are a number of different Greek words used in the Bible for "will." The Greek word used in the thirteenth verse, "... nor of the will of the flesh," implies desire or anticipation but not determination. This usage is wonderful, far beyond what we realize when first reading it. "Which were [Who was] born not of blood, nor of the will [determination] of the flesh, nor of the will [determination] of man ...." Man might desire or anticipate the Christ, but man could never determine Jesus Christ's birth. Man could not say,

"Now I am going to produce the Christ," because Jesus Christ was not born according to the determination of the flesh ...." Every woman had the physical potential to bring forth Jesus Christ; but the will of a human being could not determine the coming of Jesus the Christ because He was born by the will, the determining, of God.

> John 1:14:
> And the Word [revealed Word, Jesus Christ] was made flesh [the conception], and dwelt among us [his birth], (and we beheld his glory, the glory as of the only begotten of the Father,) full of grace and truth.

The "word" is again the *logos,* which had been in God's foreknowledge since before the foundation of the world, later being revealed to man as the spoken and written Word throughout the Old Testament. Verses 1—13 deal specifically with the time from before the foundation of the world through the events of the Old Testament as people looked toward the coming of the incarnate Word which was not seen until Jesus Christ was born. Then verse 14 declares that the Word was made flesh. In other words, the Word became incarnate.

The verb "was made" is *egeneto*, as in verse 3. Again this verb is in the aorist tense indicating the singleness of the action: Jesus Christ came once and for all.

He did not come on a number of occasions, but one time only to redeem man. This verb form is again in the passive voice as it was in verse 3, which points out that the Word was made flesh by an outside source. In this case it is God. In order for one thing to be made by another, a difference in the two things is implied. Jesus Christ the Son of God was made by God. This substantiates what was clearly stated in verse 3 that all things were made by God. And without Him was nothing made that was made or that does exist even in the present. The Word which was in God's foreknowledge at this moment in time was made flesh by God. His spoken Word by the angel Gabriel was announced to Mary and the incarnate Word became flesh when seed was created in Mary. At that moment, God created the sperm, which genetically contained soul-life, that impregnated Mary's egg or ovum. And so the Word, Jesus Christ, was made flesh by God.

The word "flesh" is the Greek word *sarx*. The natural human being is composed of flesh (*sarx*) and blood (*haima*), that is body and soul.[11] When Jesus Christ was born, the flesh was a result of Mary's egg and God's created sperm combining. However, the soul-life which is found in the blood is determined entirely by the sperm. It is the blood which directs the activities of the

---

11. Hebrews 2:14: "Forasmuch then as the children are partakers of flesh and blood, he also himself likewise took part of the same; that through death he might destroy him that had the power of death, that is the devil.

flesh. As the soul prospers, so the body prospers.[12] When the Word became flesh it was the soul-life created in the womb of Mary that made the difference between Jesus Christ the Son of God and all other sons of God.

The comma following the word "flesh" represents a period of nine months or a human gestation period. The Word began to be made flesh when God created the sperm in Mary. But that new life did not dwell among the people until a period of nine months later when Jesus Christ was born.

The word "dwelt" is the Greek word *eskēnōsen*. It comes from the noun *skēnē* which means "a tent or tabernacle." Our human bodies are spoken of in the Scriptures as tabernacles. A tent or tabernacle is a temporary dwelling place which is mobile. Our human bodies are only a temporary dwelling place. This world is not our permanent abode; we're just passing through. When the Word became flesh, it had a temporary dwelling place, a human body, the body of our Lord Jesus Christ. After nine months of *in utero* growth, the word lived or dwelt among the people.

When the Lord Jesus Christ was resurrected, he received a new, incorruptible body. Therefore, his first body was only a temporary dwelling place. It, the first corruptible body, dwelt among us temporarily. The word "dwelt" is in the aorist tense, again indicating sin-

---

12. III John 2: "Beloved, I wish above all things that thou mayest prosper and be in health, even as thy soul prospereth."

gleness of the action, for Jesus Christ came once and only once to save man. His redeeming work has been accomplished and completed.

The word "among" is the Greek word *en*. It is used to denote accompaniment via inclusion. In other words, "the Word" when it became incarnate dwelled in a temporary human body just as all of us. Jesus Christ was a human being, a man who had passions as we do and who was tempted in every point, yet he was without sin. He had his tent in (inclusion) and among (accompaniment with) our tents. How wonderfully God legally formed, made and created all things in order to bring about His plan of redemption of mankind after Adam's fall.

The next part of verse 14 is a parenthesis which is a figure of speech in which additional material is added to the text: "(and we beheld his glory, the glory as of the only begotten of the Father.) The word "beheld" is the Greek word *etheasametha* which means "to behold," "observe" or "visualize," but not necessarily with the physical eye. For example, we may observe or visualize another person's interest in what we are saying, not with our physical eyes but by certain other signs that we perceive in observing them.

The word "glory" is *doxa*, meaning "brightness." The brightness of the sun and the moon is clearly seen with the physical eyes, but not all brightness or glory is seen as physical. It may be something which is felt or known by the things that are seen. "And we beheld or perceived, though not with the physical eyes, his glory or brightness which was felt and known by the things which he did while he was here upon the earth."

Verse 14 goes on to say that this glory or brightness was as of an only-begotten of a father. The glory of a father is always seen in his son. A son innately tends to reflect his father. The word "of" which precedes "a father" is the Greek word *para* used with a noun in the genitive case and should be translated "from beside" indicating motion from the side of, as a tangent proceeding from the top of a circle. This further indicates the distinction between the Father and Son rather than the two being one and the same: "a glory as of an only begotten from beside a father."

The last five words in verse 14 are outside of the parenthesis and refer back to the Word which had its temporary dwelling place among us in God's Son, Jesus Christ. He was "full of grace and truth." Before the accomplishments of Jesus Christ, the law had to be kept by man for his salvation. But when Jesus Christ came, God showed the fullness of His grace or divine favor to man by making known to man the great breadth of His love.

"We beheld [intently observed] his [Jesus Christ's] glory [brightness], the glory as of the only begotten of the Father." Jesus Christ always did the will of the

Father.[13] Jesus Christ in the flesh declared God unto mankind.[14] Jesus Christ, the promised One, was the only-begotten of the Father because God only once created soul-life in the womb of a woman.

Verses 15-17 are truly parenthetical and further elaborate upon verse 14.

John 1:15—17:
John bare witness of him, and cried, saying, This was he of whom I spake, He that cometh after me is preferred before me: for he was before me.

And of his fulness have all we received, and grace for grace.

For the law was given by Moses, *but* grace and truth came by Jesus Christ.

Verse 15 says that Jesus was preferred before John. Jesus Christ was preferred before John because John was an Israelite and Israel was first "called in Jacob";[15]

---

13. John 4:34: "Jesus saith unto them, My meat is to do the will of him that sent me, and to finish his work."
John 6:38: "For I came down from heaven, not to do mine own will, but the will of him that sent me."
John 8:29: "And he that sent me is with me: the Father hath not left me alone; for I do always those things that please him."
Luke 2:49: "And he said unto them, How is it that ye sought me? wist ye not that I must be about my Father's business?"
14. I John 1:2: "For the life was manifested, and we have seen *it*, and bear witness, and shew unto you that eternal life, which was with the Father, and was manifested unto us."
15. Genesis 35:10-12: "And God said unto him, Thy name *is* Jacob: thy name shall not be called any more Jacob, but Israel shall be thy name: and he called his name Israel.
And God said unto him, I *am* God Almighty: be fruitful and multiply; a

Jesus Christ had already been called in God's foreknowledge from the beginning. Jesus Christ came after John in the sense that John was six months old when Jesus was born.

Verse 16:
And of his fulness have all we received, and grace for grace.

The word "fulness" is *plērōmatos* meaning "filled to capacity." It is out of his complete fullness that we were filled to capacity when we were born again of God's Spirit and received Christ in us. The word "received" is from the root *lambanō* which means "to receive to the end that we manifest that which is received." We not only received the fullness of Christ in us, but we also receive him into manifestation as we walk on God's Word and exercise the power of God's gift, holy spirit.

The word "for" is *anti,* meaning "against." So the last phrase should read "... even grace against grace"; that is, grace is piled up against grace. There is no grace like God's divine favor in what He made available through His Son, Jesus Christ, which is Christ in you, the hope of glory.

---

nation and a company of nations shall be of thee, and kings shall come out of thy loins;
And the land which I gave Abraham and Isaac, to thee I will give it, and to thy seed after thee will I give the land."

Verse 17:

For the law was given by Moses, *but* grace and truth came by Jesus Christ.

Verse 17 terminates the parenthesis made up of verses 15, 16 and 17 with the reiteration of the latter part of verse 14: "for the law was given by Moses, *but* grace and truth came by Jesus Christ." When the Word was made flesh, the incarnate Word then fully declared this grace and truth.

These first 17 verses span all that transpired from before the beginning, through the Old Testament, through the life of Christ, culminating in the riches of the mystery which Jesus Christ made available by his accomplishment.

John 1:18:

No man hath seen God at any time; the only begotten Son, which is in the bosom of the Father, he hath declared [*exēgeomai*, made known] *him.*

Verse 18 forms the great summary and contains the purpose for all that transpired in the first 17 verses.

This climaxing verse of the first part of the Gospel of John begins in the English with the words "no man." In Greek these words are the one word *oudeis* which means "not one" or "no one" -- no one without exception, like the "all" without exception in verse 3. Absolutely no one without any exceptions has seen God at any time. God is Spirit[16] and God is invisible.[17] Therefore, man with his physical eyes cannot see, hear, smell, taste or touch God who is Spirit. Man can only see the manifestation of God in the senses realm. For example, in the Old Testament Moses was able to see the burning bush. The people of Israel were able to see the tables of stone. Similarly, in the book of Daniel, the king was able to see the handwriting on the wall. It is impossible for any man to physically see God since God has neither form nor substance of the senses realm; God is Spirit.

The words "hath seen" are the one Greek word *heōraken* which occurs here in the perfect tense, active voice. The perfect tense is normally indicative of past action with the effect or result in the present time. However, it is occasionally used as a figure of speech, *heterosis,* for a pluperfect tense. The figure of speech *heterosis,* meaning "another" or "different," affects the meaning of words or a change of syntax and rhetoric.

The specific *heterosis* figure used in verse 18 is called *enallage. Enallage* is the change of one part of speech for another such as a verb would change its tense, mood or person or a noun could change its case. *Heterosis* is the name given to that figure consisting of an exchange of parts of speech by accident, and that is where the perfect is used for the pluperfect as in John 1:18. This

---

16. John 4:24: "God *is* a Spirit; and they that worship him must worship *him* in spirit and in truth."

17. I Timothy 1:17: "Now unto the King eternal, immortal, invisible, the only wise God, *be* honour and glory for ever and ever. Amen.

figurative usage of the Greek perfect tense occurs else-where.

> Acts 7:35:
> This Moses whom they refused, saying, Who made thee a ruler and a judge? the same did God send *to be* a ruler and a deliverer by the hand of the angel which appeared to him in the bush.

The words "did send" are in the perfect tense (liter-ally "has sent"), but should read in the pluperfect tense, according to the figure of speech *heterosis*, "had sent."

> Romans 16:7:
> Salute Andronicus and Junia, my kinsmen, and my fellow-prisoners, who are of note among the apostles, who also were in Christ before me.

The word "were" in the above verse is in the perfect tense (literally "have been"), but should read in the pluperfect tense, according to the figure *heterosis*, "had been."

> Hebrews 7:6,9:
> But he whose descent is not counted from them received tithes of Abraham, and blessed him that had the promises.
>
> And as I may so say, Levi also, who received tithes, paid tithes in Abraham.

In these two verses in Hebrews, the word "received" is in the perfect tense (literally "has received"), but should read in the pluperfect tense "had received."

Hebrews 8:5:
Who serve unto the example and shadow of heavenly things, as Moses was admonished of God when he was about to make the tabernacle: for, See, saith he, *that* thou make all things according to the pattern shewed to thee in the mount.

The words "was admonished" in this verse are in the perfect tense (literally "has been admonished"), but should read in the pluperfect tense, by the figure *heterosis,* "had been admonished."

Thus the statement in verse 18, "No man hath seen God," according to the figure *heterosis,* should read, "No man had seen God." The perfect tense is "hath seen God," but the figure of speech throws the tense back in time to the pluperfect, "had seen" instead of "hath seen."

Up to and unto this point, absolutely no one *had* perceived God to the extent that Jesus Christ declared Him. With the coming of Jesus Christ, God's only-begotten Son, God's grace and truth was shown in a fuller capacity than it had ever been before.

Therefore John 6:46 can say,

Not that any man hath seen the Father, save he which is of God, he hath seen the Father.

Since grace and truth did not come in an abundant capacity until Jesus Christ, the people in Old Testament times did not as fully perceive God. Christ perceived God to a greater extent than any other person ever had.

The expression that no man hath seen God at any time is again found in I John 4.

I John 4:12 and 13:
No man hath seen God at any time. If we love one another, God dwelleth in us, and his love is perfected in us.

Hereby know we that we dwell in him, and he in us, because he hath given us of his Spirit.

The word "see" in this verse is *theaomai* which, as in John 1:14, could be translated "beheld," not necessarily indicating a seeing with the physical eyes but rather a perception of understanding. Here in I John it says that no one can physically see God, but we may now perceive God when the spirit from Him is born within us. Man could observe Jesus Christ who was physically present upon earth, but man can only perceive God when the spirit from God is born within him.

I Corinthians 2:9 and 10:
But as it is written, Eye hath not seen, nor ear heard, neither have entered into the heart of man, the things which God hath prepared for them that love him.

But God hath revealed *them* unto us by his Spirit: for the Spirit searcheth all things, yea, the deep things of God.

We are able to perceive God by the spirit in us which was made available by His only-begotten Son, our Lord and Savior Jesus Christ. Natural man, who does not have the spirit from God within him, cannot know God;[18] but we can, for we have His spirit by which He may reveal Himself to us.

John 5:37:
And the Father himself, which hath sent me, hath borne witness of me. Ye have neither heard his voice at any time, nor seen his shape.

The word "to see" in this verse is again a form of the word *horaō,* which means "to perceive or understand as a result of that which is seen." Before Christ, no one perceived the Father in such fullness; after Christ's baptism, he alone was able to perceive the greatness of Him.

John 14:8 and 9:
Philip saith unto him, Lord, shew us the Father, and it sufficeth us.

---

18. I Corinthians 2:14: "But the natural man receiveth not the things of the Spirit of God: for they are foolishness unto him: neither can he know *them,* because they are spiritually discerned."

> Jesus saith unto him, Have I been so long time with you, and
> yet hast thou not known me Philip? he that hath seen me hath
> seen the Father; and how sayest thou *then,* Shew us the
> Father?

Again the words translated "to see" in these verses
are forms of *horaō.* What Jesus was saying to Philip in
the latter verse was that anyone who has really under-
stood what Jesus Christ was about as a result of seeing
him has been able to perceive the Father also. Since it
clearly says in I Timothy 1:17 that God is invisible, it is
apparent that no one could physically see God at any
time; yet people were able to perceive Him as a result of
the Word made incarnate, God's Son, Jesus Christ. If
you are able to perceive the Son, you are able to perceive his Father. A school teacher many times knows
much about the things that happen with the parents at
home because of the way the son or daughter conducts
himself or herself in school. So it is with God and His
Son.

> John 1:18:
> No man hath seen God at any time; the only begotten Son,
> which is in the bosom of the Father, he hath declared *him.*

The next part of this verse reads "... the only begotten Son ...." The Greek words are *ho monogenes huios.*
Ho is the article bringing a special emphasis to his being
the only-begotten Son. *Monogenes* is a combination of

the word *monos* which means "only" and *genos* which means "offspring," "nation," "race" or "family." (English derives the word "gene" directly from *genos.* Christ was genetically God's only Son.) Literally this word means "only offspring" or "only begotten." The usage of this Greek word in the New Testament is always found in the context of one and only one offspring.

In some of the ancient uncial manuscripts, the word "son" in the phrase "only-begotten Son" was changed to "God," thus reading "only-begotten God." However, the majority of uncials, Aramaic and other manuscripts corroborate the reading "Son" which fits with all related scriptures. To understand how the word "God" replaced "Son" in some manuscripts, we must know how errors come about. A scribe just having copied verse 14 which reads "the only begotten of the Father" could easily have carried the same thinking into verse 18 and transcribed the verse to read "the only begotten of God," which would later be altered to read "the only-begotten God." This kind of error in which one passage is assimilated to the wording of a similar passage is not uncommon.[19]   On the other hand, the error in John 1:18 could have been an intentional change due to the doctrinal error propounded as early as the second century.

To be in harmony with all related scriptures, the pre-

19. Another clear-cut example of passage assimilation is Colossians 1:4 in which the words "through his blood" were added in some of the later manuscripts to agree with Ephesians 1:7.

ferred text reads "son." The rendition given in the King James Version stands the test of the manuscripts; it should read and does read "... the only begotten Son..."[20]

The next section of verse 18 reads "... which is in the bosom of the Father ...."

. "In the bosom" is an Oriental idiom meaning "love, comfort and rest."[21] Jesus Christ was in the bosom of the Father, not by pre-existence, but in the foreknowledge of God. Jesus Christ, the only-begotten Son, was in the love, comfort and rest of the Father who knew all from the beginning. Jesus Christ then made known the Father.

... he hath declared *him.*

The word "he" is the Greek word *ekeinos,* a demonstrative pronoun pointing out the Son who is the only begotten and who is in the bosom of the Father. Literally it reads "that one." In other words, "that One has declared him."

The word "declared"[22] in Greek is *exegesato.* It is a combination of the two words *ek* which means "out" or "out from" and *hegēomai* which means "to lead."

20. The words "only begotten" are used six times in the Bible referring to Jesus Christ. Five times it says, "only begotten Son" (John 1:18, John 3:16, John 3:18, Hebrews 11:17, I John 4:9) and once it says "only begotten of the Father" (John 1:14).
21. Note II Samuel 12:3; Isaiah 40:11; Luke 16:22; John 13:23.
22. Other usages of this word "declare" include Acts 10:8; 15:12, 14, 21:19.

Literally, this word means "to lead out" which is to declare or unfold that which has been concealed. *Exegesato* is in the aorist tense indicating again the singleness of the action. It was a one-time event. When Christ came the first time, he came once and one time only to declare or unfold the Father who had been concealed, for no one previously had been able to perceive God in such greatness. When Christ comes the second time, he will not come to declare the Father but to judge mankind according to the previous declaration.

An English word which is derived from this Greek word *exegesato* is "exegesis," a term used in religious contexts regarding the declaration of scriptures or the making known of scriptures by unfolding their meaning to others. Since no one was able to perceive in such fullness the greatness of God before Christ came, Christ came to declare or unfold more fully the Father to us. Since Christ's resurrection and the day of Pentecost, we are able to have Christ within us when we are born again. Then we too may perceive God and declare Him to all men. This is our ministry of reconciliation.

In a study on "Who Is the *Logos,* the Word," in addition to the opening verses in the Gospel of John, we must also consider the following scriptures.

As noted previously, Jesus Christ's existence began when God created the sperm with soul-life in Mary.

John 3:13:
And no man hath ascended up to heaven, but he that came down from heaven, *even* the Son of man which is in heaven.

"Came down from heaven" was the conception or creation of life in Mary for the Son of God. The last four words in the verse are to be deleted as they are not in the oldest extant manuscripts. [23]

Colossians 1:14-18 contains a figure of speech which must be carefully noted for a clear understanding of God's Word.

Colossians 1:14 and 15:
In whom [Jesus Christ] we have redemption through his blood, *even* the forgiveness [*asphesin,* remission] of sins:

Who [Jesus Christ] is the image of the invisible God, the first-born of every creature.

God is invisible because He is Spirit. Jesus Christ was visible; he was, therefore, by his example in his physical body showing forth the image of God who is Spirit.

Verses 16 and 17 of Colossians 1 form a parenthesis which is a figure of speech explaining in more detail one point in the text. When a parenthesis is employed, one must proceed in reading from the last word preceding the parenthesis to the first word after the parenthesis.

---

23. P46, P45, A, L.

No thought continuity is lost, and the truth is quickly evident.

Reading from the last word of verse 15 directly on to verse 18 without reading the parenthesis of verses 16 and 17 will give the following statement:

Who [Jesus Christ] is the image of the invisible God, the first born of every creature.

And he [Jesus Christ] is the head of the body, the church ....

The parenthetical verses 16 and 17 refer to what God did.

For by him [God] were all things created, that are in heaven, and that are in earth, visible and invisible, whether *they be* thrones, or dominions, or principalities, or powers: all things were created by him [God], and for him [God] :

And he [God] is before all things, and by him [God] all things consist [cohere, were created] .

The people who say that all things were created by Jesus Christ contradict the first verse of the Bible: "In the beginning God created ...."

Another example of a stumbling block is found in John 10:30 where Jesus says, "I and *my* Father are one." It has already been established that Jesus and God are not one from the beginning, but they were one in purpose as shown in the context of this verse as Jesus

declared His Father on earth. God and Jesus Christ's
unanimity of purpose is poignantly shown in that Jesus
Christ always did the Father's will.[24] and finished the
work for which God had sent him.[25]

Hebrews 1 contains another erroneously interpreted
passage which must be rightly divided in our study.

Hebrews 1:1 and 2:

God, who at sundry times [various times] and in divers
[varied] manners [ways] spake in time past unto the fathers
by the prophets.

Hath in these last days [in this last time] spoken unto us by
his Son, whom he [God] hath appointed heir of all things, by
[for] whom also he made the worlds.

---

24. John 4:34: "Jesus saith unto them, My meat is to do the will of him
that sent me, and to finish his work."

John 5:30: "I can of mine own self do nothing: as I hear, I judge: and
my judgment is just; because I seek not mine own will, but the will of the
Father which hath sent me."

John 6:38: "For I came down from heaven, not to do mine own will, but
the will of him that sent me."

25. Hebrews 12:2: "Looking unto Jesus the author and finisher of *our*
faith; who for the joy that was set before him endured the cross, despising
the shame and is set down at the right hand of the throne of God."

John 5:36: "But I have greater witness than *that* of John: for the works
which the Father hath given me to finish, the same works that I do, bear
witness of me, that the Father hath sent me."

John 17:4: "I have glorified thee on the earth: I have finished the work
which thou gavest me to do."

John 19:30: "When Jesus therefore had received the vinegar, he said, It is
finished: and he bowed his head, and gave up the ghost."

See Chapter Two for a fuller examination of Jesus Christ.

Originally God created all things to His own satisfaction, knowing in His foreknowledge that His only-begotten Son would enjoy those things which God had created for Himself and for His appointed heir. The Greek word for "by" is *dia,* and, in the genitive case, is translated "on account of" or "because of" or, according to current language, "for." "Worlds" is the Greek word *aion* meaning "ages." God appointed His Son heir of all things, for whom also He made the ages. God structured the ages because of the need for the redemptive work of Christ.

Ephesians 3:9 contains a snag which came about because of the Stephens text.

Ephesians 3:9:
And to make all *men* see what *is* the fellowship [*oikonomia,* administration] of the mystery, which from the beginning of the world hath been hid in God, who created all things by Jesus Christ.

The words "by Jesus Christ" are in only *one* critical Greek text, Stephens; therefore the weight of the evidence demands that those three words be deleted. Truly, God created all things.

Christians who believe the Bible and who rightly divide it know that God is the Word, whom Jesus Christ declared. When we study the Word closely, we see how emphatically the Word corroborates itself. Instead of stumbling over scriptures, we see by careful scrutiny the precision with which God has revealed Himself to us in His Word. All Scripture — including Genesis 1:1; Genesis 1:26; John 1:1-18; John 10:30; Colossians 1:14-18; Hebrews 1:1,2; Ephesians 3:9 — reveals the light which dispels darkness regarding the truth of one God and His only-begotten Son, Jesus Christ.

CONCLUSION

The Bible, which is God's revealed Word and will, does not once mention the word "trinity," although biblically there are three: (1) God, who is Holy Spirit, the Father of our Lord Jesus Christ, (2) Jesus Christ, the Son of God, and the son of man, and (3) the holy spirit, God's gift, which God made available on the day of Pentecost.

Because God, the Father of our Lord Jesus Christ, holds an exclusive, unparalleled position, it is imperative that our worship of Him be directed to that position.

God is before everything.

Isaiah 43:10:
Ye are my witnesses, saith the Lord, and my servant whom I have chosen: that ye may know and believe me, and under-

stand that I *am* he: before me there was no God formed, neither shall there be after me.

God is the most holy.

I Samuel 2:2:
There is none holy as the Lord: for *there is* none beside thee: neither *is there* any rock like our God.

God has no equal.

Deuteronomy 32:39:
See now that I, *even* I, am he, and *there is* no god with me ....

God alone holds the power of salvation.

Isaiah 43:11:
I, *even* I, *am* the Lord; and beside me *there is* no savior.

God does not want His people to know or worship any other gods.

Hosea 13:4:
Yet I *am* the Lord thy God, from the land of Egypt, and thou shalt know no god but me: for there is no savior beside me.

Exodus 20:3:
Thou shalt have no other gods before me.

The unique and exalted position of God as one God is taught throughout the Word. Thus we must worship God as the one and only God. What does God's revelation of Himself in His Word say? This only is true and right doctrine.

HOLY SPIRIT

One of the most misunderstood fields among Christians today is that of the Holy Spirit. Since it is germane to this work on a study of God and the Son of God, let's very briefly get an over-view of the Holy Spirit. God is Holy and God is Spirit. The gift that He gives is holy spirit.

First of all we must note that in the Greek manuscripts and texts the word *pneuma,* "spirit," is never capitalized. Therefore, when the word *pneuma* is translated "Spirit" with a capital "S" or "spirit" with a small "s," it is an interpretation and, as such, is of no higher authority than the person or translator giving it.

By recognizing this practice, it is understandable why so many people confuse the Giver, Holy Spirit, with the gift, holy spirit. The Giver is God who is Spirit, *pneuma,* and Holy, *hagion*.[1] God, who is the Holy Spirit, can only give that which He is. Therefore, the gift of the Giver is of necessity holy, *hagion,* and spirit, *pneuma.*

> Luke 11:13:
> If ye then, being evil, know how to give good gifts unto your children: how much more shall your heavenly Father give the Holy Spirit [*pneuma hagion*] to them that ask him?

This verse clearly shows that *pneuma hagion* is the gift from God the Father, therefore, should be translated with a small "h" and a small "s." The gift is not the Giver, and the Giver is not the gift.

Another example of the difference between the Giver and the gift is found in the third chapter of John.

> John 3:6:
> .... that which is born of the Spirit [the *pneuma,* Spirit, God] is spirit [*pneuma,* gift] .

check
to v

In this passage we find Jesus talking to Nicodemus, a Pharisee, at which time the new birth was not available. It became available on the day of Pentecost. In the new birth, man receives spirit from God who is the Spirit. Again it is possible to see the important difference between the gift and the Giver.

Still another good illustration of the difference be-

---

1. John 4:24: "God *is* a Spirit: and they that worship him must worship *him* in spirit and in truth."

tween the Giver, God, and the gift is found in John 14.

John 14:16,17,26:
And I will pray the Father, and he shall give you another Comforter, that he may abide with you for ever;

Even the Spirit of truth; whom the world can not receive, because it seeth him not, neither knoweth him: but ye know him; for he dwelleth with you, and shall be in you.

But the Comforter, *which is* the Holy Ghost, whom the Father will send in my name, he shall teach you all things, and bring all things to your remembrance, whatsoever I have said unto you.

In the Old Testament and the Gospels, we find that men of God have the spirit upon them. We also find that these men operated seven manifestations of the spirit which were prophecy, word of knowledge, word of wisdom, discerning of spirits, faith, miracles and healing. Jesus told the disciples that the holy spirit was *with* them and *upon* them and that at a future time it would be *in* them. The reason the gift, *pneuma hagion,* was not in them was that it was not yet available for them to be born again.

John 7:39:
(But this spake he [Christ] of the Spirit, which they that believe on him should receive; for the Holy Ghost [the gift, holy spirit] was not yet *given;* because that Jesus was not yet glorified.)

The new birth was not available until the day of Pentecost. This can be seen in the twenty-fourth chapter of Luke.

Luke 24:49:
And, behold, I send the promise of my Father upon you: but tarry ye in the city of Jerusalem, until ye be endued with power from on high.

Jesus commanded his disciples to wait in Jerusalem until they received the gift which was promised from the Father, that being *pneuma hagion.* Another illustration of this is found in Acts.

Acts 1:4 and 5:
And, being assembled together with *them,* commanded them that they should not depart from Jerusalem, but wait for [until] the promise of the Father, which, *saith he,* ye have heard of me.

For John truly baptized with water; but ye shall be baptized with the Holy Ghost not many days hence.

We can see in these passages that the gift, *pneuma hagion,* is referred to by several different terms: the comforter, power from on high, the promise of the Father, to be baptized with the holy spirit.

Now let's read the account of Pentecost.

Acts 2:1-4:
And when the day of Pentecost was fully come, they [twelve apostles] were all with one accord in one place.

And suddenly there came a sound from heaven as of a rushing mighty wind, and it filled all the house where they were sitting.

And there appeared unto them cloven tongues like as of fire, and it sat upon each of them.

And they were all filled with the Holy Ghost [*pneuma hagion*], and began to speak with other tongues, as the Spirit [the *pneuma*] gave them utterance.

In these four verses, we have the complete record of the receiving of the gift, *pneuma hagion,* power from on high, by twelve apostles. The speaking in tongues was the external manifestation of the receiving of the gift of holy spirit. In Mark 16:17, Jesus says that believers in His name "shall [absolutely] speak with new tongues." The new birth was available for the first time with Pentecost.

After the twelve apostles were born again and spoke in tongues, Peter stood and taught the multitudes. At the conclusion of his message, he taught them how to receive the new birth and speak in tongues.

Acts 2:38 and 39:
Then Peter said unto them, Repent, and be baptized every one

of you in the name of Jesus Christ for the remission of sins, and ye shall [absolutely] receive [*lambanō*,manifest] the gift of the Holy Ghost.

For the promise is unto you, and to your children, and to all that are afar off, *even* as many as the Lord our God shall call.

The promise of the Father was now available to everyone who believed according to Romans 10:9 and 10.

That if thou shalt confess with thy mouth the Lord Jesus, and shalt believe in thine heart that God hath raised him from the dead, thou shalt be saved.

For with the heart man believeth unto righteousness; and with the mouth confession is made unto salvation.

When people believed, they were born again and received *pneuma hagion,* power from on high. The gift of *pneuma hagion* was in them and sealed them forever as stated in Ephesians.

Ephesians 1:13:
In whom ye also *trusted,* after that ye heard the word of truth, the gospel of your salvation: in whom also after that ye believed, ye were sealed with that holy spirit of promise.

The greatness of God's revealing Himself to the Church of grace was brought about by the accomplishments of Jesus Christ. For after Jesus Christ was sacrificed, was resurrected and then ascended, it was possible for God to send His gift which dwells permanently in all believers. The communication between God and man was holy spirit which came from God, *pneuma hagion*, Holy Spirit.[2]

---

2. See Victor Paul Wierwille, *Receiving The Holy Spirit Today* (American Christian Press, New Knoxville, Ohio, 1972).

COMMON ERRORS IN UNDERSTANDING

Many scriptures have been wrongly used to substantiate the doctrine of "God the Son" by not adhering to the fundamental principles of biblical interpretation. This chapter lists the more prominent misunderstandings, followed by their clarifications.

Exodus 3:14:
And God said unto Moses, I AM THAT I AM: and he said, Thus shalt thou say unto the children of Israel, I AM hath sent me unto you.

The expression in the Hebrew literally reads "I will be what I will be." There was no pronounceable name for the true God, in contrast to the pagans who always called their gods by name.

Psalm 2:7:
I will declare the decree: the Lord hath said unto me, Thou *art* my Son; this day have I begotten thee.

Psalms 2 was *prophetical,* looking forward to the first and second comings of Christ.

Psalms 110:1,4:
The Lord said unto my Lord, Sit thou at my right hand, until I make thine enemies thy footstool.

The Lord hath sworn, and will not repent, Thou *art* a priest for ever after the order of Melchizedek.

This entire psalm is prophetical, looking forward to the redeeming work of Christ.

Psalms 130:7 and 8:
Let Israel hope in the Lord: for with the Lord *there is* mercy, and with him *is* plenteous redemption.

And he shall redeem Israel from all his iniquities.

The word "hope" in verse 7 is the key. Hope is used regarding that which is future. Israel awaited the coming of the redeeming Messiah. They looked forward to his first coming, just as we look forward to his second.

Isaiah 40:3:
The voice of him that crieth in the wilderness, Prepare ye the way of the Lord, make straight in the desert a highway for our God.

This prophetical statement signifies that John came to make straight the way of God. Jesus Christ was God's plan for man's redemption. John was a servant of God, not of Christ. This same situation arises in Matthew 3:3 and John 1:23.

Matthew 3:3:

For this is he that was spoken of by the prophet Esaias, saying, The voice of one crying in the wilderness, Prepare ye the way of the Lord, make his paths straight.

John 1:23:

He said, I *am* the voice of one crying in the wilderness, Make straight the way of the Lord, as said the prophet Esaias.

The book of Daniel tells that Shadrach, Meshach and Abednego were put at the command of Nebuchadnezzar.

Daniel 3:25:

He answered and said, Lo, I see four men loose, walking in the midst of the fire, and they have no hurt; and the form of the fourth is like the Son of God.

It does not say that the fourth form *was* the son of God, only that it was *like* the son of God. The usage of "like" makes this expression a simile, a figure of speech, which is not literal.

Matthew 1:21,23:

And she shall bring forth a son, and thou shalt call his name JESUS: for he shall save his people from their sins.

Behold, a virgin shall be with child, and shall bring forth a son, and they shall call his name Emmanuel, which being interpreted is, God with us.

Names given to Christ such as *Jesus,* meaning "God our Savior," and *Emmanuel,* meaning "God with us," emphasize his service to mankind. They do not indicate that Jesus is God any more than Joshua's name, meaning "God our Savior," signifies that Joshua was God or that a girl named Barbara means she is a barbarian.

Matthew 12:31 and 32:
Wherefore I say unto you, All manner of sin and blasphemy shall be forgiven unto men: but the blasphemy *against* the *Holy* Ghost shall not be forgiven unto men.

And whosoever speaketh a word against the Son of man, it shall be forgiven him: but whosoever speaketh against the Holy Ghost, it shall not be forgiven him, neither in this world, neither in the *world* to come.

The Holy Spirit is God.[1] Verse 32 clearly indicates a difference between God and His Son.

Matthew 22:44:
The Lord said unto my Lord, Sit thou on my right hand, till I make thine enemies thy footstool?

Ephesians 4:5 says there is one Lord and one God. Jesus Christ is our Lord, but God is his Lord or Master.

---

1. See Appendix A.

Luke 2:11:
For unto you is born this day in the city of David a Saviour, which is Christ the Lord.

Christ is our Lord. God is Lord over all. Compare I Corinthians 15:27,28; John 14:28; I Corinthians 8:6 and I Corinthians 11:3.

Luke 3:21 and 22:
Now when all the people were baptized, it came to pass, that Jesus also being baptized, and praying, the heaven was opened,

And the Holy Ghost descended in a bodily shape like a dove upon him, and a voice came from heaven, which said, Thou art my beloved Son; in thee I am well pleased.

In these verses the distinction between God, His Son, and the spiritual ability Christ received from God is clear.

Luke 18:18 and 19:
And a certain ruler asked him, saying, Good Master, what shall I do to inherit eternal life?

And Jesus said unto him, Why callest thou me good? none *is* good, save one, *that is,* God.

This verse clearly shows Jesus correcting the ruler for calling him "good master."

John 3:13-15:
And no man hath ascended up to heaven, but he that came down from heaven, *even* the Son of man which is in heaven.

And as Moses lifted up the serpent in the wilderness, even so must the Son of man be lifted up:

That whosoever believeth in him should not perish, but have eternal life.

The oldest extant manuscripts delete the last four words in verse 13, "which is in heaven." The son of man came down by God's miraculous conception.[2] Verses 14 and 15 clarify the time of his ascension as being future. Christ was talking to Nicodemus regarding what would become available in the future.

John 5:17-19:
But Jesus answered them, My Father worketh hitherto, and I work.

Therefore the Jews sought the more to kill him, because he not only had broken the sabbath, but said also that God was his Father, making himself equal with God.

Then answered Jesus and said unto them, Verily, verily, I say unto you, The Son can do nothing of himself, but what he seeth the Father do: for what things soever he doeth, these also doeth the Son likewise.

---

2. See Chapter Three, pages 71-74.

The Son could only walk with the power and authority of his Father, as belonging to him, if he obeyed and carried out what his Father said. The context makes the distinction between Father and Son clear.

John 5:23:
That all *men* should honour the Son, even as they honour the Father. He that honoureth not the Son honoureth not the Father which hath sent him.

If someone did not respect your son, you too might be insulted and disturbed.

John 6:20:
But he saith unto them, It is I; be not afraid.

"It is I" is "I am" in the Greek. This no more shows that Jesus Christ is God than my saying "I am" proves that I am God.

John 8:58:
Jesus said unto them, Verily, verily, I say unto you, Before Abraham was, I am.

Christ was with God in His foreknowledge before Abraham was born. Compare notes on Exodus 3:14. John 9:9 and John 18:6 contain the same common error in understanding.

John 9:9:
Some said, This is he: others *said,* He is like him: *but* he said, I am *he.*

John 18:6:
As soon then as he had said unto them, I am *he*, they went backward, and fell to the ground.

The expression "I am" is not singularly used of God.

John 12:38-41:
That the saying of Esaias the prophet might be fulfilled, which he spake, Lord, who hath believed our report? and to whom hath the arm of the Lord been revealed?

Therefore they could not believe, because that Esaias said again.

He hath blinded their eyes, and hardened their heart; that they should not see with *their* eyes, nor understand with *their* heart, and be converted, and I should heal them.

These things said Esaias, when he saw his glory, and spake of him.

Isaiah saw Christ in prophetic revelation. He looked forward to the coming of the Christ.

John 14:1,8,9,16:
Let not your heart be troubled: ye believe in God, believe also in me.

Philip saith unto him, Lord, shew us the Father, and it sufficeth us.

Jesus said unto him, Have I been so long time with you, and yet hast thou not known me, Philip? he that hath seen me hath seen the Father; and how sayest thou *then,* Shew us the Father?

And I will pray the Father, and he shall give you another Comforter, that he may abide with you for ever.

These verses clearly show the Father, His Son, and the gift of holy spirit, not as identities, but as three working in unison with singleness of purpose.

In examining John 16:13 and 15, carefully note the pronoun "he."

John 16:13 and 15:
Howbeit when he, the Spirit of truth, is come, he will guide you into all truth: for he shall not speak of himself; but whatsoever he shall hear, *that* shall he speak: and he will shew you things to come.

All things that the Father hath are mine: therefore said I, that he shall take of mine, and shall shew *it* unto you.

All the pronouns "he" referring to the spirit are masculine to agree with the word "comforter." This word comforter is a descriptive word used in place of the word "spirit" and grammatically pronouns must agree in gender with the noun to which they are related. In Greek the gender of a word does not necessarily denote the actual gender of the object. If this verse

h.s.
properly
said ref as
neuter

really meant that the spirit is masculine (and therefore a person and part of the trinity), what about Romans 8:26 where the pronoun "itself" which refers back to "spirit" is the *neuter* form. Therefore, John 16:13 and 15 do *not* prove the holy spirit is part of the trinity.

John 16:27-30:
For the Father himself loveth you, because ye have loved me, and have believed that I came out from God.

I came forth from the Father, and am come into the world: again, I leave the world, and go to the Father.

His disciples said unto him, Lo, now speakest thou plainly, and speakest no proverb.

Now are we sure that thou knowest all things, and needest not that any man should ask thee: by this we believe that thou camest forth from God.

There have been many others sent forth from God but none were conceived of God as Jesus was in Mary. See chapter 3, pages 71-74.

Acts 2:34:
For David is not ascended into the heavens: but he saith himself, The Lord said unto my Lord, Sit thou on my right hand.

Ephesians 4:5 says there is one Lord and one God. Jesus Christ is our one Lord, but God is his Lord or Master. Compare this with the note on Psalms 110:1.

Also see I Corinthians 11:3.

Acts 7:37-39:
This is that Moses, which said unto the children of Israel, A prophet shall the Lord your God raise up unto you of your brethren, like unto me; him shall ye hear.

This is he, that was in the church in the wilderness with the angel which spake to him in the mount Sina, and *with* our fathers: who received the lively oracles to give unto us:

To whom our fathers would not obey, but thrust *him* from them, and in their hearts turned back again into Egypt.

The pronoun "he" in verse 38 refers to Moses, not Christ.

Acts 7:59:
And they stoned Stephen, calling upon *God,* and saying, Lord Jesus receive my spirit.

The Critical Greek texts contain no word "God" in the above. The Greek texts read, "And they stoned Stephen, invoking and saying, Lord Jesus, receive my spirit." The Aramaic texts also omit "God."

Galatians 4:6:
And because ye are sons, God hath sent forth the Spirit of his Son into your hearts, crying, Abba, Father.

In one of the earliest extant manuscripts of the New Testament, one at the Chester Beatty Papyrii known as P^{46} (c. 200 A.D.), the word "son" is deleted. The manuscript reads, " . . . God has sent forth His spirit into your hearts ...."

Colossians 1:13:
Who hath delivered us from the power of darkness, and hath translated *us* into the kingdom of his dear Son:

Verse 14:
In whom we have redemption through his blood, *even* the forgiveness of sins:

Verse 15:
Who is the image of the invisible God, the firstborn of every creature:

Verse 16:
For by him were all things created, that are in heaven, and that are in earth, visible and invisible, whether *they be* thrones, or dominions, or principalities, or powers: all things were created by him, and for him:

Verse 17:
And he is before all things, and by him all things consist.

Verse 18:
And he is the head of the body, the church: who is the beginning, the firstborn from the dead; that in all things he might have the preeminence.

Verse 15 says that "his dear Son" is the first born of every creature. Then verses 16 and 17 are a parenthesis (*parembole,* which is a figure of speech) in which the insertion is complete in itself explaining God as the Creator. Verse 18 picks up from verse 15 to speak about Christ as the head of the body. See chapter 3.

Colossians 2:9:
For in him dwelleth all the fulness of the Godhead bodily.

God was in Christ. Colossians 1:27 says that Christ is in us. This does not make us Christ or God.

I Thessalonians 3:11:
Now God himself and our Father, and our Lord Jesus Christ, direct our way unto you.

The first connective "and" is *kai* in Greek and is often translated "even." Then it would read, "Now God himself even our Father."

I Timothy 2:3:
For this *is* good and acceptable in the sight of God our Saviour.

God is our Savior as the *author* of the plan of salvation. Jesus Christ made the new birth available as the *agent* of the plan of salvation and as the finisher of faith.

Titus 1:3:
But hath in due times manifested his word through preaching, which is committed unto me according to the commandment of God our Saviour.

Again, God is our Savior as the *author* of the plan of salvation. Jesus Christ made the new birth available as the *agent* of the plan of salvation, the finisher of faith. This situation arises elsewhere in Titus 3:4 and in Jude, verse 25.

Titus 3:4:
But after that the kindness and love of God our Saviour toward man appeared ....

Jude 25:
To the only wise God our Saviour, *be* glory and majesty, dominion and power, both now and ever. Amen.

God is the author of salvation.

Titus 2:13:
Looking for that blessed hope, and the glorious appearing of the great God and our Saviour Jesus Christ.

Jesus Christ is part of the glory of his Father. In all Critical Greek texts and extant manuscripts this verse literally reads, "Looking for that blessed hope and appearing of the glory of the great God even our Saviour Jesus Christ." The glory of the great God is His Son.

Hebrews 1:2:
Hath in these last days spoken unto us by *his* Son, whom he hath appointed heir of all things, by whom also he made the worlds.

The word "worlds" is the word *aion* which means "ages." It was because of Christ's redemptive works that God structured the various ages to fulfill his redemptive plan. See chapter 3.

Hebrews 1:10:
And, Thou, Lord, in the beginning hast laid the foundation of the earth; and the heavens are the works of thine hands.

"And, Thou, Lord" addresses God who is the Creator of the heavens and the earth according to Genesis 1:1.

I John 5:20:
And we know that the Son of God is come, and hath given us an understanding, that we may know him that is true, and we are in him that is true, *even* in his Son Jesus Christ. This is the true God, and eternal life.

The word "even" is in italics indicating that it appears in no text. The words "him that is true" are two Greek words, literally translated, "the true." "True" is an objective used here as a noun and as such is translated "true one." In other words the verse reads: "And we know that the Son of God is come, and hath given us an understanding that we may know the true One [God;

John 1:18], and we are in the true One [God] by the work of his Son Jesus Christ. This [the true One] is the true God who is eternal life."

SCRIPTURES REFERRING TO GOD AND HIS SON

I n this appendix are listed primary scriptures dealing with God and His Son Jesus Christ.

Matthew

    3:17: . . . my beloved Son in whom . . .

    4:3: . . . thou be the Son of God . . .

    4:6: . . . thou be the Son of God . . .

    8:29: . . . Jesus, thou Son of God . . .

    14:33: . . . of a truth thou art the Son of God.

    16:16: . . . the Son of the living God.

    17:5: . . . my beloved Son in whom . . .

    26:63: . . . Christ, the Son of God.

    27:40: . . . the Son of God.

    27:43: . . . I am the son of God.

    27:54: . . . this was the Son of God.

Mark

1:1: . . . Jesus Christ, the son of God.

1:11: . . . my beloved son, in whom . . .

3:11: . . . Thou art the Son of God.

5:7: . . . Jesus, thou Son of the most high God.

9:7: . . . This is my beloved son . . .

15:39: . . . this man was the Son of God.

Luke

1:32: . . . called the Son of the Highest . . .

1:35: . . . the Son of God.

3:22: . . . my beloved son in thee . . .

4:3: . . . thou be the Son of God . . .

4:9: . . . thou be the Son of God . . .

4:41: . . . Thou art Christ the Son of God.

8:28: . . . Jesus, thou son of God most high.

9:35: . . . my beloved son . . .

John

1:18: . . . no man hath seen God . . . the only begotten son . . . hath declared him.

1:34: . . . this is the Son of God.

1:49: . . . thou art the Son of God.

3:16: . . . God . . . gave his only begotten son . . .

3:17: . . . God sent . . . his son . . .

3:18: . . . the only begotten son of God.

5:25: . . . the son of God . . .

6:69: . . . Christ, the son of the living God.

9:35: . . . the son of God.

10:36 . . . I am the Son of God.

11:4: . . . that the son of God . . .

11:27: . . . Christ, the son of God . . .

19:7: . . . himself, the son of God . . .

20:31: . . . the Christ, the Son of God . . .

Acts

8:37: . . . I believe that Jesus Christ is the Son of God.

9:20: . . . that he is the Son of God.

13:33: Thou art my Son . . .

Romans

1:3: . . . Son, Jesus Christ our Lord . . .

1:4: . . . declared to be the Son of God . . .

1:9: For God . . . of his Son

5:10: . . . to God by the death of his son . . .

8:3: . . . God sending his own son . . .

I Corinthians

1:9: God . . . of his Son Jesus Christ . . .

II Corinthians

1:19: . . .For the Son of God, Jesus Christ . . .

Galatians

2:20: . . . by the faith of the Son of God . . .

4:4: . . . God sent forth his son . . .

Ephesians
4:13: . . . knowledge of the Son of God . . .

I Thessalonians
1:9,10 . . . the living and true God and . . . his
Son . . . Jesus . . .

Hebrews
4:14: . . . Jesus the Son of God . . .
6:6: . . . the Son of God . . . .
7:3: . . . the Son of God . . .
10:29: . . . the Son of God . . .

I John
1:3: . . . Father, and with his Son Jesus Christ.
3:8: . . . the Son of God . . .
4:15: . . . Jesus is the Son of God . . .
5:5: . . . Jesus is the Son of God?
5:10: . . . the Son of God . . . God gave of his Son.
5:12: . . . the Son of God . . .

5:13: . . . the Son of God . . .
5:20: . . . the Son of God . . . his Son Jesus Christ . . .

II John
3: . . . God the Father, and from the Lord Jesus
Christ, the Son of the Father . . .

SCRIPTURES REFERRING TO CHRIST'S CONCEPTION AND BIRTH

I n this appendix are listed all scriptures found in the New Testament dealing with the following words: beget, begotten, born, conceived, created, made, man and son in reference to the Lord Jesus Christ. Also are included the corresponding Greek words, from which the English was translated, with their meanings.

A. Words concerned with the conception and birth of the Lord Jesus Christ.
   1. beget – Greek *gennaō* -- bring forth, come into existence. Acts 13:33; Hebrews 1:5; 5:5; I John 5:1.
   2. begotten (only) – Greek *monogenēs* – only born. John 1:14,18; 3:16,18; Hebrews 11:17; I John 4:9.

3. begotten (first) – Greek *protōtokos* – first born. Hebrews 1:6.

4. born – Greek *gennaō* – to beget, bring forth. Matthew 1:16; 2:1,4; Luke 1:35; John 1:13; 18:37.

5. conceive – Greek *gennaō* – to beget, bring forth. Matthew 1:20.

6. conceive – Greek *sullambanō* – to receive (seed). Luke 1:31; 2:21.

B. The use of the words "created" and "made" in reference to the Lord Jesus Christ.

1. created – Greek *ktizō* – to produce, bring into being. Colossians 3:10.

2. made – Greek *ginomai* – to begin to be, to come into existence, or into any state, as implying origin. John 1:14; Romans 1:3; I Corinthians 15:45; Galatians 4:4; Philippians 2:7; Hebrews 1:4; 6:20; 7:16.

C. The use of the word "man" in reference to the Lord Jesus Christ.

1. man – Greek *anēr* – an adult male person. John 1:29,30; Acts 2:22 – twice.

2. man – Greek *anthrōpos* – a human being. Matthew 8:9 (in the Greek texts it reads: "For I also am a man"); 8:27; 26:72,74; Mark 14:71; 15:39; Luke 7:8; 23:4,6,14 – twice, 47; John

4:29; 5:12; 7:46,51; 9:11,16,24; 10:33; 11:47,50; 18:14,17,29; 19:5; Acts 4:12; 5:28; Romans 5:19 (suggested from context); I Corinthians 15:21,47; Galatians 3:15; Ephesians 3:16; 4:24; Philippians 2:7,8; I Timothy 2:5.

3. man — Greek *arrhen* — a male or the male sex. Revelation 12:5.

D. The use of the word "son" in reference with the Lord Jesus Christ.

1. son — Greek *pais* — a child. Acts 3:13,26.

2. son — Greek *teknon* — that which is born, a child. Luke 2:48.

3. son — Greek *huios* — son, descendent, offspring, (reference is made to the origin or starting point of and to the relation in which he stands). Matthew 1:21,23,25; 2:15; 3:17; 11:27; 13:55; 16:16; 17:5; 22:42,45. Mark 2:10; 5:7; 6:3; 9:7; 12:37; 13:32. Luke 1:31,32; 2:7; 3:22; 4:22; 9:35; 10:22. John 1:18,45; 3:16,17,35,36; 5:19,20,21,22,23,25,26; 6:40,42; 8:35,36; 14:13; 17:1. Acts 13:33. Romans 1:3,9; 5:10; 8:3,29,32. I Corinthians 1:9; 15:28. II Corinthians 1:19. Galatians 1:16; 2:20; 4:4,6. Colossians 1:13. I Thessalonians 1:10. Hebrews 1:2,5,8; 3:6; 5:5,8; 7:28. II Peter 1:17. I John 1:3,7; 2:22,23,24; 3:23; 4:9,10,14; 5:9,10,11,12,20. II John 3,9.

4. Son (Greek *huios* – see D-3) of[1] David. Matthew 1:1; 9:27; 12:23; 20:30,31; 15:22; 21:9,15; 22:42. Mark 10:47,48; 12:35. Luke 18:38,39; 20:41,44.

5. Son (Greek *huios* – D-3) of[1] God. Matthew 4:3,6; 8:29; 14:33; 26:63; 27:40,43,54. Mark 1:1; 3:11; 15:39. Luke 1:35; 4:3,9,41; 8:28; 22:70. John 1:34,49; 3:18; 5:25; 6:69; 9:35; 10:36; 11:4,27; 19:7; 20:31. Acts 8:37; 9:20. Romans 1:4. II Corinthians 1:19. Galatians 2:20. Ephesians 4:13. Hebrews 4:14; 6:6; 7:3; 10:29. I John 3:8; 4:15; 5:5,10,12,13,20. Revelation 2:18.

6. Son (Greek *huios* -- See D-3) of[1] man (Greek *anthropos* – see C-2) Matthew 8:20; 9:6; 10:23; 11:19; 12:8,32,40; 13:37,41; 16:13,27,28; 17:9,12,22; 19:28; 20:18,28; 24:27,30,37,39,44; 25:13,31; 26:2,24,45,64. Mark 2:10,28; 8:31,38; 9:9; 12:31; 10:33,45; 13:26; 14:21,41,62. Luke 5:24; 6:5,22; 7:34; 9:22,26,44,58; 11:30; 12:8,10,40; 17:22,24,26,30; 18:8,31; 19:10; 21:27,36; 22:22,48,69; 24:7. John 1:51; 3:13,14,18; 5:27; 6:27,53,62; 8:28; 12:23,34; 13:31. Acts 7:56. Hebrews 2:6. Revelation 1:13; 14:14.

---

1. The word "of" in these verses is in the genitive case and, in this case, it is the genitive of origin meaning the source from which anything has its origin. Therefore it can be translated "from."

The use of these words demonstrates the fact that Jesus Christ was "begotten" and, therefore, was not "from the beginning." He was not the alpha as God is the Alpha and Omega.

Sources used in this appendix: Robert Young, *Young's Analytical Concordance to the Bible;* E. W. Bullinger, *A Critical Lexicon and Concordance.*

APPENDIX E

LISTING OF SCRIPTURES

B [handwritten, next to Isaiah]

Mt5 but I say... [handwritten note]

B 11. 28,29 [handwritten]
(169) [handwritten]

(Handwritten marginal annotations present throughout, including: "come down fr heaven", "from God seen Father", "6.62", "help the of God", "B7.28 sent – others", "29", "PreEx", "B8.18 sent", "sent me", "el am 8.24 el am", "Faith into of X", "10.29-33 'make yourself God'", "B10.38 sent", "B11.42 43", "who comes into world", "B12.44 49 50", "He that has seen me...", "B14.12 ?", "see Athanasius Ar & Calvin", "came from – going to", "came from God", "I am come forth from...", "whom thou hast sent", "6.50 6.51 came down from heaven", "B Rev 13.?, B blasph")

B P hil 2

Col 1.16,17

_26_

_2.2_

_3:10 p 158_

_8 2 Th 1.12_

_2 Th. 1.12_

noth. in Rev!

RESOURCES

Our source of study was the Bible. However, 428 other books are in a bibliography. If you would like a copy of this, please write, addressing your letter to The Way International, Box 328, New Knoxville, Ohio 45871.

ABOUT THE AUTHOR

Dr. Victor Paul Wierwille, moving into his fourth decade of biblical research and teaching, has witnessed countless occasions when Christians as a united body could stand together as the light of the world. But, because of multiple, divisive doctrines believers have decimated their message. "The church will not again have the power and influence God intended," Dr. Wierwille believes, "until the born-again believers stop fighting each other and fight the Adversary."

In his search to strip modern Christianity of many centuries of tradition and take a pure look at God's revealed Word, Dr. Wierwille founded and is currently president of a research, teaching and training ministry called "The Way." This rapidly expanding diverse group of people believe that the Bible in its original, first text is the Word of God; it alone can set men free and bring unity to God's people.

In his many years of research, Dr. Wierwille has studied with such men as Karl Barth, E. Stanley Jones, Glen Clark, Bishop K.C. Pillai and George M. Lamsa. His formal training includes a Bachelor of Divinity from Mission House (Lakeland) College and Seminary. He studied at the University of Chicago and at Princeton Theological Seminary from which he received a Master of Theology. Later he completed his work for the Doctor of Theology degree.

"When we as workmen rightly divide the Word of God," Dr. Wierwille stresses, "then the Christian Church will not only have the power demonstrated by the first-century Church, but even more important, we will stand approved before God as faithful and good workmen." This research work, *Jesus Christ Is Not God*, is another contribution toward rightly dividing God's Word and thereby being able to live the more abundant life which Jesus Christ made available.